THE CHATGPT ALCHEMIST

13 Ways to Make Money with ChatGPT

Felix Venture

Table of Contents

YOUR FREE BONUSES.. 9

INTRODUCTION 11

    What is ChatGPT.. 11

    Choosing Between ChatGPT-4 and GPT-3.5............. 12

    How to Get the Most Out of This Book 14

    Limitations and Responsible Use of ChatGPT......... 17

CHAPTER 1: CONTENT CREATION 20

    Leveraging ChatGPT for Content Creation.............. 20

    Practical Tips for Crafting Content with ChatGPT... 22

    Diversifying Your Content 24

    Quality vs. Quantity 25

    Strategic Marketing 27

CHAPTER 2: SPEECH WRITING 31

    Crafting Speeches with ChatGPT 31

    The Elements of Effective Speechwriting 33

    Tailoring Speeches to Audiences and Occasions 35

    Practical Tips for Speechwriting with ChatGPT....... 37

    Marketing Speechwriting Services 39

CHAPTER 3: E-LEARNING CONTENT CREATION 43

    Developing E-learning Courses with ChatGPT 43

    Educational Principles and Learning Styles 45

Practical Tips for E-learning Content Creation........ 48

Ensuring Content Quality and Educational Value ... 50

Marketing and Selling E-learning Content 51

CHAPTER 4: SEO OPTIMIZATION 57

Crafting SEO-Optimized Content with ChatGPT 57

In-depth Keyword Research for SEO 59

SEO Strategies and Keyword Integration 61

Analytics and Performance Tracking....................... 63

Practical Tips for SEO Optimization with ChatGPT.. 64

CHAPTER 5: RESUMES AND COVER LETTERS 69

Drafting Resumes and Cover Letters with ChatGPT 69

Recruitment Landscape and Employer Expectations 72

Maintaining Professionalism and Accuracy 74

Practical Tips for Resumes and Cover Letters Creation 76

Marketing Resume Services to Job Seekers............. 79

CHAPTER 6: EMAIL MARKETING 83

Email Content and Newsletters with ChatGPT 83

Email Marketing Strategies and Best Practices....... 86

Offering Email Marketing Services.......................... 88

Analyzing Performance and Optimizing for Conversions 90

Automated Email Responses and Customer Interaction 91

CHAPTER 7: WEBSITE COPYWRITING 96

Creating Website Copy with ChatGPT 97

The Principles of Effective Web Copywriting 99

Offering Web Copywriting Services 101

Optimizing Web Copy 103

Challenges and Solutions in Web Copywriting 105

CHAPTER 8: PRODUCT DESCRIPTIONS 109

Crafting Product Descriptions with ChatGPT 109

E-commerce Trends and Consumer Behavior 112

Offering Product Description Services 114

Optimizing Product Descriptions 116

Practical Tips for Product Description Writing with ChatGPT 118

CHAPTER 9: TRAVEL BLOGS AND GUIDES 122

Creating Content for Travel Blogs with ChatGPT .. 122

Travel Trends and Audience Preferences 124

Diversifying Content to Cover Various Travel Destinations 126

Ensuring Accuracy in Travel Content 128

Practical Tips for Travel Content Creation with ChatGPT 130

CHAPTER 10: SCRIPT WRITING 135

Drafting Scripts with ChatGPT 135

Scriptwriting for Different Platforms 139

Creativity and Originality in Scriptwriting............. 141

Practical Tips for Scriptwriting with ChatGPT 144

CHAPTER 11: AD COPYWRITING 149

Drafting Ad Copies with ChatGPT 149

Advertising Principles and Consumer Psychology 150

Offering Ad Copywriting Services 154

Optimizing Ad Copy for Conversion....................... 157

Practical Tips for Ad Copywriting with ChatGPT... 159

CHAPTER 12: SOCIAL MEDIA MANAGEMENT........... 164

ChatGPT for Social Media Content Creation.......... 164

Maintaining a Consistent Brand Voice................... 166

Offering Social Media Management Services....... 167

Engagement and Community Management.......... 169

Practical Tips for Social Media Management with ChatGPT 172

CHAPTER 13: LANGUAGE TRANSLATION 178

Leveraging ChatGPT for Translation Services......... 178

Selection of Language Pairs and Niches 180

Ensuring Accuracy and Cultural Appropriateness. 182

Practical Tips for Translating Content with ChatGPT 184

    Marketing Translation Services.............................. 186

THANK YOU... 190

CONCLUSION 192

    Ethical and Responsible Use of AI in Business...... 192

    Future Prospects: The Evolving Landscape of AI .. 194

    Call to Action: Your Next Steps 196

    Embracing Digital Alchemy to Unlock New Opportunities 198

Copyright © 2024 Felix Venture. All rights reserved.

Notice of Rights

No part of this book may be reproduced, stored in a retrieval system, or transmitted in any form or by any means, electronic, mechanical, photocopying, recording, scanning, or otherwise, except as permitted under Section 107 or 108 of the 1976 United States Copyright Act, without the prior written permission of the publisher. Reviewers may quote brief passages in reviews.

Disclaimer

This book is intended for informational and educational purposes only and is not a substitute for professional financial advice. The author and publisher are not responsible for any actions taken by the reader. The information in this book is provided on an "as is" basis with no guarantees of completeness, accuracy, usefulness, or timeliness. Under no circumstances will any blame or legal responsibility be held against the publisher, or author, for any damages, reparation, or monetary loss due to the information contained within this book. Either directly or indirectly. You are responsible for your own choices, actions, and results.

Brand names, products, and services mentioned in this book are used for identification purposes only and do not imply endorsement. All trademarks and registered trademarks appearing in this book are the property of their respective owners. The publishers and the book are not associated with any product or vendor mentioned in this book. None of the companies referenced within the book have endorsed the book.

YOUR FREE BONUSES

A Special Thank You to My Readers

As a token of my appreciation for your purchase, I am excited to offer not just one but two exclusive bonuses designed to add practical value to your journey and help you maximize your learnings from this book.

1. "Quick Start Guide: How to Create Your Custom GPT": This eBook is a concise guide tailor-made to help you kickstart your journey with ChatGPT. The guide provides step-by-step instructions and screenshots to help you create your very own custom GPT model.

2. "Customizable ChatGPT Templates": This eBook contains a carefully crafted template for each of the business ideas discussed in my book. The templates are designed to offer a solid foundation for your endeavors in various domains. Each template is a tool for efficiency and effectiveness, empowering you to implement the strategies and insights from the book with precision and creativity.

These bonuses are my way of saying thank you for joining me on this inspiring journey. They are investments in your potential, aiding you in unlocking the full power of ChatGPT to revolutionize your online earning endeavors.

Happy reading, and here's to your success in mastering digital alchemy with ChatGPT!

Get your free gifts here: https://bit.ly/4cUyEoM
Alternatively, scan the QR code below:

INTRODUCTION

What is ChatGPT

ChatGPT is a remarkable example of artificial intelligence (AI), seamlessly integrating advanced technology with natural conversation. It's an advanced **language model** created by OpenAI that understands and generates text so human-like that you might forget you're talking to a machine.

Imagine chatting with a knowledgeable companion who is always ready to answer your questions, assist in your writing projects, and serve as your brainstorming partner. ChatGPT is that digital ally, harnessing the raw power of GPT (**Generative Pretrained Transformer**) models to cultivate meaningful dialogues.

GPT models are trained on a vast ocean of internet text. This enables ChatGPT not just to echo the information it's been trained on but to interpret your input, understand the context, and formulate relevant and coherent responses.

But why is ChatGPT a game-changer in our quest for digital alchemy? It's your trusty sidekick, ready to lend a hand to everyone from entrepreneurs to content creators. Think of it as a digital assistant that helps sharpen your ideas, weaves compelling stories, and concocts practical solutions.

Throughout this book, you'll discover how ChatGPT is transforming the landscape of online income generation. It can help you write top-notch blog posts, craft engaging e-learning materials, and much more. It's a game-changer for individuals and businesses, opening up a world of possibilities.

Choosing Between ChatGPT-4 and GPT-3.5

As we navigate the ever-changing landscape of artificial intelligence, the choice between ChatGPT-4 and GPT-3.5 becomes crucial. These two versions offer distinct features and capabilities tailored to different needs.

Key Differences:

- **Model Complexity:** GPT-4, with its approximately 1.76 trillion parameters, surpasses GPT-3.5's 175 billion, enabling more refined and contextually aware responses.

- **Processing Speed and Creativity:** GPT-4 offers improved processing speed and excels in creative writing, while GPT-3.5 provides basic creative content generation.

- **Data Analysis:** GPT-4 advances in providing in-depth data analysis, whereas GPT-3.5 offers fundamental data analysis capabilities.

- **Coding Assistance:** GPT-4 is proficient in software development support, outperforming GPT-3.5's basic coding assistance.

- **Visual Comprehension:** Unique to GPT-4, it can comprehend and process visual information, a feature absent in GPT-3.5.

- **Pricing:** GPT-3.5 is free, while GPT-4 requires a subscription, currently $20/month, reflecting its advanced capabilities.

With regard to practical applications, both models are versatile, but GPT-4's enhancements significantly broaden its applicability, offering advanced solutions for complex problems and creative tasks.

Decision Guidance:

- **GPT-4** is the go-to choice for those seeking the utmost AI capabilities and willing to invest in a subscription for the most advanced features.

- **GPT-3.5** remains a compelling option for those on a budget or who need a simple tool without GPT-4's full suite of features.

When deciding between Chat GPT-4 and GPT-3.5, consider your profession, preferences, budget, and project requirements.

How to Get the Most Out of This Book

This book is designed to show you how ChatGPT can be a valuable asset in generating income online. It excels in various tasks essential for digital success, providing a strong foundation for those looking to strengthen their online presence and excel in the content creation industry.

We'll explore 13 different ways to earn money online using ChatGPT. But to truly harness the wealth of opportunities presented here, I encourage you to keep an open mind about the various ways you can monetize the consistent stream of high-quality content that ChatGPT helps create. Beyond directly offering your skills as a service to potential clients, consider also sponsored posts, affiliate marketing, and even paid subscriptions to premium content. Or maybe you could launch your own faceless YouTube channel.

By the end of the book, we'll ensure you're well-prepared for your digital journey, from understanding the requirements of each of the 13 avenues to marketing them effectively. Each chapter is enriched with real-life examples, practical advice, and step-by-step guides, along with exercises to sharpen your skills.

Please note that I'll share some prompts for engaging with ChatGPT, but I won't give you the outputs directly. I encourage you to try them yourself and see the possibilities unfold. Each concept we'll discuss is an invitation to dive deeper, learn, and grow. You cannot become a master in a field by treading on the surface; genuine expertise calls for immersion.

Besides this, it's essential to have a strong foundation in how ChatGPT works and the art of crafting effective prompts. For this purpose, I wrote another book called "ChatGPT for Beginners: Prompt Engineering Made Easy." This companion book is designed to enhance your understanding and interaction skills with ChatGPT, which is crucial for leveraging the 13 monetization strategies outlined here. Understanding ChatGPT and mastering prompt engineering are the keys to unlocking the full potential of the methods discussed. ChatGPT's capabilities are vast, but tapping into them requires knowing how to ask the right questions and frame prompts to elicit the most useful responses.

Why is this important? The effectiveness of the monetization strategies detailed here is significantly amplified when you're proficient in prompt engineering. When you interact with ChatGPT, the quality of your input directly influences the quality of the output. By first grounding yourself in the foundational principles and techniques of working with ChatGPT, you ensure you're well-equipped to apply these skills across various monetization methods.

Since it was not possible to condense all the information into a single volume, this book focuses on presenting 13 strategies for making money online with ChatGPT, while "ChatGPT for Beginners" is dedicated to the technical skills needed to make those strategies work. Together, they offer a comprehensive roadmap for anyone looking to explore ChatGPT's potential for online entrepreneurship.

Limitations and Responsible Use of ChatGPT

When using ChatGPT, it's crucial to recognize its limitations and advocate for responsible use. Despite being an impressive example of artificial intelligence, it comes with its own challenges and responsibilities that users must be aware of.

Understanding without Consciousness: It generates responses based on patterns in its training data, which can sometimes produce inaccurate or sensitive outputs.

Temporal Knowledge Limit: Its knowledge was frozen in April 2023, making it unaware of events or developments that have occurred since.

Contextual Limitation: Because it has a limited context window, it can lose track of extended conversations, leading to responses that may deviate from the intended context.

Simulated Creativity: While it can generate creative content, its creativity is simulated and may not always produce truly novel or abstract ideas.

Absentee Ethical Compass: It lacks a moral or ethical compass. It can provide information on ethical principles but doesn't inherently understand or apply them.

Dependency on User Input: The quality of ChatGPT's responses is directly related to the clarity of the user's queries. Vague questions can lead to vague answers.

Credibility and Bias Concerns: Its responses can reflect the biases or inaccuracies in the data on which it was trained.

Inability to Learn or Remember: It can't learn from interactions or remember past engagements.

Legal and Ethical Boundaries: It operates within legal and ethical limits and cannot engage in illegal activities, provide professional advice, or partake in harmful behaviors.

ChatGPT is a powerful tool but not a substitute for human knowledge; I'll stress this a lot in the book. It bridges human creativity and technological capability, serving as an assistant rather than a replacement.

Understanding ChatGPT's limitations and advocating for responsible use is essential if you want to leverage its capabilities effectively. Whether you're an aspiring content creator, marketer, or business owner, AI can be a formidable ally in digital productivity, but only when used appropriately. The onus is on us, the users, to use it responsibly and ethically.

CHAPTER 1: CONTENT CREATION

Leveraging ChatGPT for Content Creation

ChatGPT can generate a wide array of content, from insightful blog posts to engaging social media updates. Its expansive knowledge base and adaptive algorithms allow it to mimic various writing styles, adapt to different tones, and cater to multiple niches. Whether you want to craft concise, compelling social media posts or develop in-depth, informative articles, this AI can be molded to fit your unique content requirements.

However, the key to unlocking ChatGPT's full potential lies in your ability to guide it effectively. Despite its ability to produce text based on the data it has been trained on, it lacks genuine understanding or consciousness, so you must ensure the content it produces is accurate, authentic, and original. Strategies such as refining your initial instructions, customizing the generated outputs, and integrating unique, brand-specific elements can significantly enhance the originality and authenticity of the content.

You should also always tailor your content to specific audiences and niches. This involves deeply understanding your target demographic's preferences, pain points, and interests. The goal is to direct ChatGPT in producing content that engages the intended audience and offers them real value. For instance, if you're targeting a tech-savvy audience, you might guide ChatGPT to produce content that delves into the intricacies of the latest technological advancements. On the other hand, if the audience comprises lifestyle enthusiasts, it can be directed to create content that focuses on wellness, fashion, or travel.

The versatility of this tool also extends to content formats. Beyond traditional articles and blog posts, you can leverage ChatGPT to create newsletters, eBooks, or even video scripts. Each format offers a unique way to engage with a specific audience and can be optimized for different platforms and purposes. For example, a well-crafted newsletter can be a powerful tool for customer retention, while an eBook can be an excellent lead magnet.

Practical Tips for Crafting Content with ChatGPT

ChatGPT is a game-changer for content creators, but let's be honest: owning a Swiss Army knife doesn't make you a survivalist. Mastery comes from knowing how to use your tools effectively. When it comes to ChatGPT, this mastery is achieved through the precision of your prompts and the diligence of your refinements.

When crafting prompts, it's important to **be specific**. Think of ChatGPT as a tool that requires clear instructions to produce the desired output. A broad prompt like "*Write *about healthy living*" is too general. Instead, detail your request:

Example Prompt:

"*Write a 600-word blog post on the benefits of a plant-based diet for young professionals interested in fitness, keeping a motivational tone.*"

This specificity guides ChatGPT in generating content that aligns more closely with your vision.

The **refinement** stage is crucial for ensuring the generated content meets your standards. ChatGPT can create content quickly, but your role is to refine this output. Check for factual accuracy, narrative flow, and relevance to your target audience. Iteratively revise and adjust the content until it reaches the quality that resonates with your readers.

Be mindful of ChatGPT's **limitations**. Its knowledge is up to date until April 2023. Additionally, due to its limited context window, it might not fully grasp lengthy discussions. Understanding these constraints is key to creating effective prompts that maximize ChatGPT's strengths while minimizing its weaknesses.

Diversifying Your Content

In a world where content is the currency, diversification is your investment strategy. With ChatGPT as your versatile sidekick, you can immerse yourself in many content niches and platforms. The goal is simple: create content that attracts attention while inspiring action.

The first step is **niche research**. The landscape of content niches, from technology and business to lifestyle and fashion, is vast and varied, with each sector presenting its unique characteristics and audience expectations. While ChatGPT can mimic the required language, tone, and style for each niche, your expertise and understanding of the niche augment the depth and authenticity of the content.

Similarly, each content **platform**, be it blogs, social media, newsletters, or video scripts, operates under its own rules and audience preferences. Understanding these platforms can transform your content strategy, allowing you to tailor your messages to maximize engagement. ChatGPT's flexibility means it can adjust to these varied requirements, but your strategic insight and creative planning will define your content.

Experimentation plays a pivotal role in content diversification. Exploring different content formats and stylistic approaches keeps your audience engaged and opens new avenues for connection and impact. The objective is to refresh your content strategy continuously, keeping it dynamic and responsive to your audience's evolving needs.

Your content strategy should remain agile, ready to adapt to shifting market trends and audience preferences. Staying informed and proactive in adjusting your approach is key to maintaining relevance and engagement in the ever-changing digital landscape.

Quality vs. Quantity

The digital landscape is hungry for new, compelling content but is also picky, expecting quality and relevance. This section will guide you through this delicate balance, ensuring your content production is prolific and high-quality.

While churning out content *en masse* with ChatGPT is tempting, it is crucial to ensure that each piece is accurate, relevant, and valuable to your audience. Quality should never be sacrificed for the sake of quantity.

Quality content engages your audience and encourages interaction and sharing across multiple platforms. This, in turn, increases your brand's visibility and credibility. A well-written blog post that is rich in valuable insights and presented engagingly is more likely to be shared widely, thereby increasing your digital footprint.

When balancing quality and quantity, the focus should always be on maintaining high standards while adhering to a consistent production schedule. This might mean reducing the content volume and investing more time and resources to enhance its quality. A well-planned content calendar that aligns with your capabilities and client/audience expectations can help you achieve this balance.

Remember that not all content needs to explore a topic in depth. A strategic mix of high-quality, detailed pieces combined with shorter yet still valuable and relevant content can keep your audience engaged while you establish your authority in the field.

Balancing quality and quantity in content production is a skill that takes practice and a deep understanding of your brand and audience. When done right, your content becomes a powerful tool that enhances your digital presence.

Strategic Marketing

Even the most compelling content needs a well-thought-out marketing strategy to reach its intended audience. This section will guide you through the steps to effectively market your content services, from identifying your target audience to leveraging testimonials and case studies to establish credibility. Most of these principles can also be used to market and sell the other business ventures discussed in this book, so be creative and keep an open mind!

Any effective marketing strategy starts with a deep understanding of your **target market**. Knowing who needs AI-generated content and why enables you to customize your marketing messages to address specific pain points. Whether you're targeting small businesses needing consistent blog posts or influencers looking for engaging social media content, a clear understanding of your audience is vital.

Once you've identified your target market, the next step is to create a **solid portfolio** that showcases your content-creation capabilities. Examples of incredible ChatGPT-generated content that you have enhanced and perfected with your unique vision and touch in the real world can speak volumes about the value you can add.

In addition, you need to establish a strong **online presence** on professional networking and freelance platforms like LinkedIn, Upwork, and Fiverr. These platforms offer different avenues for visibility and client acquisition. LinkedIn can be beneficial for B2B marketing, allowing you to share insights and case studies and connect with industry professionals. Meanwhile, Upwork and Fiverr offer a more direct route to potential clients actively seeking content creation services.

References and case studies can strengthen your credibility even more. Case studies offer a more in-depth look at the difficulties, solutions, and results connected with your services, while testimonials provide social proof. Together, they develop an engaging story that has the power to persuade potential customers.

The digital marketplace is ever-evolving, and your marketing strategies must adapt accordingly. Whether through content marketing, social media engagement, or email campaigns, maintaining a dynamic and client-centric approach is essential.

Key Takeaways from Chapter 1

- ChatGPT can produce a wide range of content types, adapting to various writing styles, tones, and niches, making it a versatile tool for content creators.

- The success of content generated by ChatGPT hinges on the specificity and clarity of the prompts given.

- The refinement process is crucial for ensuring the generated content meets quality standards, including accuracy, relevance, and originality.

- Understanding and targeting specific audiences and niches are essential for creating engaging and valuable content.

- Exploring different content platforms and formats (e.g., blogs, social media, newsletters, eBooks) allows for broader engagement.

- Maintaining high-quality standards in content production is paramount, even when aiming for high volume.

- Effectively marketing AI-generated content services requires a deep understanding of the target market, a solid portfolio, an online presence, testimonials, and case studies to establish credibility.

- Stay flexible and responsive to market trends and audience preferences, emphasizing experimentation and adjustment in content strategy and marketing approaches.

CHAPTER 2: SPEECH WRITING

Crafting Speeches with ChatGPT

Different events, from educational talks to persuasive dialogues and special celebrations, require unique emotional tones and rules. Therefore, leveraging ChatGPT's capabilities becomes a strategic advantage.

For **Informative Speeches**, the main goal is to present clear, accurate, and digestible information to your audience. **Persuasive Speeches** shift the focus towards influencing opinions and evoking emotions. When it comes to **Special Occasion Speeches**, like those at weddings or graduations, understanding the emotional and cultural context is key.

ChatGPT can generate a speech that aligns with the mood and theme you specify, but your understanding of the event's nuances and the people involved will make the speech truly memorable. As you begin crafting your speech, take a moment to ask yourself some questions to stimulate your creative process.

First, consider the core message of your speech: What is the central idea or takeaway you want your audience to remember? Then, visualize the audience: Who are they? What are their interests? What might their expectations be? How can you make your message resonate with them specifically?

Think of the initial draft from ChatGPT as the raw material. Your role is to sculpt this draft into a polished piece that connects with your audience on a deeper level. This involves fine-tuning the language for greater impact, structuring the speech to keep your audience engaged, and ensuring a seamless flow from start to finish.

In the following sections, you'll learn about the key elements that make a speech engaging and impactful and how to tailor your words for different audiences and occasions. With practical guidance on using ChatGPT for crafting speeches and insights into marketing these services, you will be equipped with the skills necessary to transform your speechwriting into a profitable venture.

The Elements of Effective Speechwriting

Speechwriting is like assembling a puzzle. Each word, sentence, and paragraph must fit perfectly to convey your message, evoke emotions, or spur action. Understanding the components that make a speech stand out is crucial to ensuring it resonates with your audience and delivers your intended message.

The **introduction** is the first impression and sets the stage for your speech. You can immediately capture your audience's attention with an intriguing anecdote, a quote, or a surprising fact that ties into your speech's theme. The aim here is to spark interest and give a glimpse into the speech's main message.

The **body** of the speech is where the essence of your message lives. It's the segment where you lay out your arguments, share stories, and unfold your purpose. Clarity and coherence are paramount here. Organize your ideas, back them up with pertinent examples or data, and maintain a logical progression. Effective transitions between points are essential for keeping your speech cohesive and impactful.

The **conclusion** is your opportunity for a memorable departure, leaving your audience with lingering thoughts, feelings, or motivations. A strong conclusion revisits key points made throughout the speech, connects them back to the opening, and often includes a call to action or a provocative final thought to leave a strong impression.

The **language** should be tailored to fit your audience's demographic, cultural, and social backgrounds, making the speech relatable and engaging. Employing rhetorical devices like repetition and analogies can enhance your speech's appeal and memorability, but they should be used judiciously.

These components are your guide for utilizing ChatGPT in speechwriting. They help you in refining AI-generated drafts into coherent and deeply impactful speeches. As a speechwriter, adhering to these key elements ensures your speech communicates effectively while leaving a lasting mark on your audience.

Tailoring Speeches to Audiences and Occasions

Just as a skilled tailor crafts clothing to fit an individual's measurements, a speechwriter tailors a speech to suit the specific needs of an audience and the context of an occasion. The art of customization lies in fine-tuning the tone, style, and content based on a deep understanding of the audience and the event.

Different occasions necessitate different approaches. A wedding speech is different from a business presentation or a political rally. The first is more emotional and personal, whereas the other two require formality and authority. For example, a keynote speech at a conference should blend expertise, inspiration, and engagement to inform and motivate the audience.

To effectively tailor your speech, first understand its **purpose**. Is your speech meant to inform, persuade, entertain, or inspire? This fundamental question directs your content, tone, and style.

Next, consider the **audience demographics** and psychographics. Age, profession, and cultural background all significantly impact how your message is received. A speech written for students will naturally differ from one written for industry professionals or a specific interest group.

When using ChatGPT for speech drafting, **detailed prompts** become invaluable. Specify the occasion, demographics of the audience, and desired outcomes. Include any themes or points that you would like to be covered. This enables the AI to generate a draft that closely matches your requirements. For example, directing it with the desired tone or specific anecdotes can significantly improve the relevance and impact of the speech.

The final, essential stage is **refinement**. This step involves reviewing and polishing the draft to ensure it captures the essence of the event, connects with the audience on a meaningful level, and achieves its intended objective.

Practical Tips for Speechwriting with ChatGPT

Words have the power to inspire change and evoke emotion. This subchapter is your roadmap to crafting compelling speeches by blending human intuition with artificial intelligence.

Tip #1: Precision in Prompting.

Think of your prompts as the blueprint for ChatGPT, guiding it to create a speech that resonates with your audience and message. For instance, if you're writing an introduction for a corporate sustainability summit, your prompt should be laser-focused, like the example below:

Example Prompt:

"Write a 1000-word opening speech for a C-suite sustainability event emphasizing the climate crisis. The target audience is [...]. The aim is to [...]. Focus on the following elements [...]. Start with an anecdote to connect with the

audience. Ask me questions if you need further details."

This clarity sets the stage for a targeted, relevant output from ChatGPT.

Tip #2: Structural Integrity.

Ensure your speech is built on an engaging introduction, an informative body, and a memorable conclusion. And if you want to add flair, use rhetorical devices like metaphors. Just remember to use them sparingly to keep your message clear.

Tip #3: Iterative Refinement.

Once ChatGPT lays the groundwork, your role is to refine, rephrase, and realign the speech to ensure it meets your objectives while striking a chord with your audience.

Tip #4: Timing and Pacing.

They are equally important. A well-paced speech captures the audience's attention. This part of speechwriting ensures your message is heard and felt, building on the foundation laid by your precise prompts and structural integrity.

Tip #5: Delivery Cues.

These subtle yet impactful stage directions guide the speaker in delivering a captivating performance. While ChatGPT scripts the lines, you must handle the pauses, emphases, and voice modulations that amplify the speech's impact.

Tip #6: Originality and Authenticity.

They are your moral compass. To ensure your speech is unique, employ plagiarism detection tools like Grammarly.

Marketing Speechwriting Services

In this section, we'll look at how to market your speechwriting services to a diverse clientele, from individuals to large corporations. What you need is a symbiotic combination of client understanding, a compelling portfolio, a strong online presence, and strategic networking.

Understanding **client needs** is the foundation of any successful marketing strategy. The world of speechwriting is a kaleidoscope of events and audiences, each requiring a unique narrative approach. Your marketing should reflect this diversity by providing tailored solutions relevant to each client's specific context and goals.

Your **portfolio** follows that. This visual resume should be a carefully curated collection of your best work, demonstrating your versatility across various occasions and audiences. If you've written speeches for high-profile events or clients, don't be afraid to use them to boost your credibility.

Your **online presence** is essentially your global stage. A clean, professional website, complemented by active social media and professional networking profiles, can be a one-stop shop for potential clients. Engage your audience with insightful content, tips, and speech samples, positioning yourself as a thought leader in speechwriting.

Finally, don't underestimate the power of **networking** and **collaboration**. Engage in online forums, join professional associations, and connect with public speaking groups. These platforms elevate your status, potentially leading to fruitful collaborations and broadening your client horizons.

When it comes to marketing communications, focus on what sets you apart—your unique approach to understanding each client's specific needs, the audience, and the occasion. Leverage testimonials and case studies as social proof to build trust and persuade potential clients of your unparalleled expertise.

Key Takeaways from Chapter 2

- Leverage ChatGPT to create speeches for different occasions, tailoring each to the specific emotional tone and rules required.

- Achieve a memorable speech by deeply understanding the event's nuances and your audience's characteristics. This knowledge guides the customization of tone, style, and content.

- Before crafting your speech, identify the central message you want to convey and consider your audience's interests and expectations to ensure your message resonates effectively.

- Use the initial draft from ChatGPT as a foundation, refine the language, structure the speech to maintain engagement, and ensure a seamless flow from beginning to end.

- Focus on creating an engaging introduction, a coherent body, and a memorable conclusion. Use language tailored to your audience's background and employ rhetorical devices judiciously.

- Adapt your speechwriting approach based on the event type and audience demographics, utilizing detailed prompts to guide ChatGPT in generating a relevant draft.

- Refine your speeches to ensure they capture the event's essence, connect with the audience meaningfully, and fulfill their intended purpose.

- Market your speechwriting services effectively by understanding client needs, showcasing a diverse portfolio, maintaining a strong online presence, and engaging in strategic networking.

CHAPTER 3: E-LEARNING CONTENT CREATION

Developing E-learning Courses with ChatGPT

When you start building an e-learning course, the curriculum is the first thing to focus on. This is the foundation upon which your entire course will be built. Think of it as the structured path that guides your learners through their educational journey.

In this chapter, I'll show you how ChatGPT can become an invaluable assistant in this initial phase. By feeding it precise guidelines and clear educational objectives, ChatGPT can help you draft curriculum outlines, create engaging learning materials, and develop effective assessment tools. This process ensures that the curriculum meets educational standards while resonating with your target audience.

The delivery of your course content also plays a critical role in maintaining learner engagement. Here, you should introduce **interactive elements**. From scenario-based learning modules and quizzes to videos, these interactive features make learning enjoyable. With tools like text-to-speech video software, you can easily create captivating videos that add depth to your courses.

Let's consider a practical example to illustrate this approach. Imagine you're creating an online digital marketing course using ChatGPT. You aim for it to be comprehensive and engaging for beginner marketers. This course could include a mix of articles, quizzes, and real-life scenarios, all generated with the help of ChatGPT. Similarly, you could create dialogues, exercises, and assessments for a language learning course to provide an immersive learning experience. The possibilities with ChatGPT are virtually endless, opening up a world of opportunities.

To make the most of your e-learning projects, start with a clear understanding of your **educational goals** and your audience's needs.

Educational Principles and Learning Styles

When crafting e-learning courses, you need to understand educational principles and diverse learning styles. Your aim should be to create learning experiences that are pedagogically sound and centered around your learners, accommodating a wide array of preferences and needs.

Utilize the **VARK model** as a guide to ensure your content appeals to every type of learner: Visual, Auditory, Reading/Writing, and Kinesthetic. With ChatGPT, you can tailor content specifically for each group. For visual learners, focus on developing materials filled with infographics and charts. For auditory learners, script engaging podcasts or dialogues, turning them into captivating audio lessons.

Integrating educational theories into your e-learning content is also pivotal. Theories such as **Constructivism**, which emphasizes the importance of learners actively constructing their knowledge, and **Cognitive Load Theory**, which focuses on efficiently using cognitive resources, should shape how you design your courses. Use ChatGPT to help align your materials with these theories, ensuring that your content encourages active learning and is structured to optimize cognitive processing.

Example Prompt:

"I'm developing an e-learning course on digital marketing for beginner adult learners. I want to use Constructivism and Cognitive Load Theory to enhance learning.

1. *__For Constructivism:__ Can you suggest interactive activities that promote active knowledge construction by relating new information to personal experiences?*

2. *__For Cognitive Load Theory:__ How can I structure these activities and the overall course content to avoid overwhelming learners, perhaps through information segmentation or visual aids?*

The goal is to create an engaging, effective learning environment for beginners. Insights on further leveraging these theories or incorporating complementary ones are also welcome."

Another critical element is **adapting content** to cater to different age groups and specific learning needs. The approach you take for a high school student who prefers more interactive and visually stimulating content will differ from that for a professional seeking concise, actionable insights.

Finally, the role of **assessment** in e-learning cannot be overstated. Assessments should not be viewed merely as a tool for measuring learning outcomes but as a vital component of the learning process. Strive to design a variety of assessment methods, ranging from straightforward quizzes to complex, scenario-based tasks. These should evaluate the learner's understanding and encourage the practical application of knowledge.

Practical Tips for E-learning Content Creation

The first step is deeply understanding the **subject matter** and the intended **learning outcomes**. You can then guide the AI to generate the initial drafts and outlines, providing a foundational structure upon which the course can be built.

Imagine you're developing an e-learning course on "*Digital Marketing Fundamentals*." To create a comprehensive outline, start by clearly defining the scope and objectives of your course. For example, you might want to cover topics like SEO, content marketing, social media strategies, and analytics. Once you have a clear vision, provide a detailed prompt.

Example Prompt:

"*I'm creating an e-learning course called 'Digital Marketing Fundamentals.' Write an outline for an introductory course covering SEO, content marketing, social media, and analytics. Suggest up to three additional topics. Ask me questions if you need more information.*"

ChatGPT will generate an initial outline that includes key topics and subtopics under each section. You can then refine this outline by asking the AI to add specific learning objectives, recommended readings, or practical exercises for each section. This method saves time and ensures that your course structure is well-organized, covering all essential aspects of digital marketing in a logical progression. Don't forget to include quizzes, polls, and interactive scenarios to ensure learners are active participants, not just passive recipients of information.

Think about creating something that resonates with learners. By making the content relatable, you facilitate better understanding and retention of the material. You could also include case studies that provide tangible and relatable instances of how the subject matter applies in real-world scenarios. Remember that you can also use ChatGPT to craft supplementary materials like summaries and key takeaways to enhance the overall learning experience and provide learners with resources for further study. After the course is live, gathering feedback for continuous improvement is essential. Create surveys and feedback forms, and remember to analyze the data to identify areas for improvement.

Ensuring Content Quality and Educational Value

Quality assurance is your primary strategy for safeguarding the integrity of your e-learning content. This involves a meticulous process of continuous review, revision, and enhancement. Early in this process, ChatGPT can assist in the creation of initial content drafts and help compile quality assurance checklists. These checklists are important for ensuring multimedia resources are accessible, the information is current and accurate, and the content aligns with the intended learning outcomes.

Another pivotal step is ensuring that your content meets **educational standards** and objectives. The aim is to design your course as a structured pathway that leads learners to achieve specific knowledge and skills. With ChatGPT, you can tailor content to these educational goals, ensuring the material covers the relevant topics and contributes to achieving the set learning objectives.

ChatGPT can also be integrated with various educational technologies, enhancing the overall learning experience. For example, by linking it with a Learning Management System (LMS), you could automate personalized learning journeys based on individual student performance and preferences. This synergy allows for a more adaptive e-learning environment, where the system dynamically adjusts the content, suggesting additional resources or remediation as needed, all through seamless API integration.

Finally, ensure the content is unbiased and inclusive, catering to many learners. Implement accessibility features, such as screen reader compatibility, and provide alternative text for images to make e-learning accessible to all students.

Marketing and Selling E-learning Content

Marketing and selling your content is as critical as creating it. The challenge is multifaceted:

you must develop high-quality, pedagogically sound content and ensure it reaches the right audience, including students, professionals, educators, and organizations, each with unique learning objectives and requirements.

The first actionable step is identifying your target audience. Knowing who you aim to reach allows you to tailor your marketing messages effectively. For instance, if you're targeting professionals looking for career advancement, you must create content highlighting how your e-learning course can provide them with the skill set they need to climb the corporate ladder.

Next, focus on crafting a compelling **Unique Value Proposition** (UVP). Your UVP should clearly articulate what sets your e-learning content apart from the competition. It should highlight the tangible benefits learners will gain and the specific problems your course aims to solve.

Leveraging established online course platforms like Udemy can also significantly amplify your reach. These platforms provide a ready-made audience actively seeking educational content, making them an ideal channel for selling your e-learning courses.

There are many other well-established online platforms where you can sell your courses, like Skillshare and LinkedIn Learning. Skillshare offers a creative and collaborative environment ideal for design, photography, and other creative arts courses. On the other hand, LinkedIn Learning is renowned for its professional development courses, making it perfect for career-oriented content. By strategically placing your courses on these platforms, you benefit from their search and recommendation engine, which can match your content with the right learners.

One last tip: understand each platform's **unique features and audience**. For example, Udemy's user base is diverse, ranging from professionals seeking skill enhancement to hobbyists exploring new interests. Tailoring your course descriptions and promotional materials to align with the platform's style and audience preferences can significantly increase the visibility and appeal of your offerings.

Key Takeaways from Chapter 3

- Create a curriculum that serves as a structured guide for your learners. Use ChatGPT to draft outlines, learning materials, and assessments that meet educational standards and resonate with your audience.

- Integrate interactive elements into your courses, such as scenario-based learning modules, quizzes, and videos, to maintain learner engagement and add depth.

- Start with clear educational goals and an understanding of your audience's needs. Then, fine-tune the curriculum and educational materials with ChatGPT.

- Create pedagogically sound experiences that cater to visual, auditory, reading/writing, and kinesthetic learners through tailored content.

- Apply educational theories like Constructivism and Cognitive Load Theory in your course design to encourage active learning and manage cognitive processing efficiently.

- Adapt content for different age groups and learning needs, using ChatGPT to generate material that ranges from interactive content for younger learners to concise insights for professionals.

- Design various assessment methods to evaluate and reinforce learner understanding and application of knowledge.

- Ensure quality assurance through continuous review, revision, and enhancement of e-learning content, using ChatGPT to assist in creating drafts and quality checklists.

- Align your content with educational standards and objectives to create a structured learning path with specific outcomes.

- Integrate ChatGPT with educational technologies like LMS for personalized learning paths, automating content adjustment based on student performance and preferences for a dynamic learning experience.

- Commit to continuous improvement and ethical content creation, focusing on unbiased, inclusive material with accessibility features to cater to diverse learners.

- Identify your target audience to tailor marketing messages effectively, highlighting the UVP of your e-learning content.

- Leverage online course platforms such as Udemy, Skillshare, and LinkedIn Learning to sell your courses. Understand each platform's unique features and audience for optimal course placement and promotion.

CHAPTER 4: SEO OPTIMIZATION

Crafting SEO-Optimized Content with ChatGPT

Crafting SEO-optimized content with ChatGPT means finding a way to please both search engines and your readers. ChatGPT helps by creating clear and interesting content with the right keywords. Exactly what your readers are looking for.

Let's talk about **structural SEO** first. It's important to organize your content well. Use main titles and subtitles to help outline your article, write in clear paragraphs, and include links to other pages on your site or to external sites. This keeps readers engaged and facilitates the understanding and ranking of your content higher in search results by search engines like Google.

Different types of content need different SEO strategies. For blog posts, use storytelling and detailed explanations with specific, long-tail keywords. For product descriptions, focus on the unique features and benefits, using keywords that buyers might search for. Landing pages should use persuasive language and keywords effectively to make visitors want to take action. ChatGPT can adjust its writing to fit each type of content.

Using keywords correctly is very important. You should put your main keyword in the title and the beginning of your content, then naturally use related keywords and synonyms throughout the text. The main goal is to write content that's easy to read and useful, ensuring it fits what your readers and search engine algorithms are looking for.

Ensure your content remains relevant and up-to-date with the latest SEO practices and user interests. Update it regularly to keep up with new SEO trends and changes in what your readers want.

In-depth Keyword Research for SEO

Keyword research is crucial for making your content findable and appealing to your audience. It goes beyond just adding keywords to your text. Instead, it's about understanding the language your audience uses when they search online. You want to discover the questions, needs, and interests that prompt people to use certain search terms.

The first step in keyword research is to determine the words and phrases your audience uses when looking for the products, services, or information you offer. Tools like SEMrush, Ahrefs, and Google Keyword Planner are helpful here. They can show you how often certain keywords are searched, how competitive they are, and what people try to find when using them.

It's also important to understand the intent behind a search. People might be looking for information, trying to get to a specific website, looking to buy something immediately, or considering a future purchase. Knowing this helps you create content that matches what your audience wants, which in turn can improve your content's rankings and make users more satisfied.

There are different kinds of keywords. **Short-tail keywords** are broad and can be very competitive but increase visibility. For example, "*running shoes*" is a short-tail keyword. **Long-tail keywords**, on the other hand, are more specific, like "*women's waterproof running shoes for winter.*" While they might have fewer searches, they can bring in an audience that's closer to making a decision or taking action.

When creating SEO-optimized content with ChatGPT, use these carefully chosen keywords in your prompts to ensure the content is well-written and search engine-friendly. However, it's important to still use keywords naturally. Putting in too many of them can make your content less enjoyable to read and might even hurt your SEO efforts.

Adding LSI (**Latent Semantic Indexing**) keywords is another useful strategy. These are terms related to your main keywords that aid search engines to better understand the context. For example, if your main keyword is "*vegan desserts*," LSI keywords could include "*plant-based*," "*dairy-free*," or "*meatless*." This approach helps ensure your content comprehensively covers the topic and aligns with what search engines and users seek.

SEO Strategies and Keyword Integration

SEO combines several key components that work together to improve your content's visibility and effectiveness. Here's how to navigate these elements:

On-page SEO focuses on the content you publish and its HTML source code, highlighting the importance of integrating keywords naturally. For instance, if "*gluten-free baking*" is your target keyword, it should fit smoothly into your content, like in the sentence: "*Explore the delightful world of gluten-free baking with our easy-to-follow recipes.*"

Off-page SEO goes beyond just your site. It includes building backlinks from trustworthy sites, increasing domain authority, and making your content easily shareable on social media. These efforts collectively enhance the reach and trustworthiness of your content, benefiting both users and search engines.

Technical SEO, often underestimated, is vital, too. It optimizes your website's backend, ensuring search engines can easily crawl and index it. This includes enhancing site speed, ensuring mobile compatibility, and using secure, accessible URLs, which help boost your site's search engine rankings.

After conducting keyword research, you can use ChatGPT to create initial drafts, weaving in your keywords naturally to maintain the content's value for the reader. Integrate keywords in a way that matches your audience's search intent, whether it aims to inform, entertain, or persuade. This approach helps draw in and keep visitors, potentially leading to higher conversion rates.

If you aim to offer SEO-optimized content services, showing a deep understanding of SEO strategies in your portfolio is crucial. Include case studies that highlight the impact of your SEO work on search rankings, web traffic, and engagement, underscoring your comprehensive approach to creating valuable and engaging user experiences.

Analytics and Performance Tracking

Understanding SEO requires a solid grasp of analytics and performance tracking. Tools like Google Analytics and Google Search Console give you valuable insights into how your strategies are working. However, you must know how to read these insights to make informed decisions.

Your website's **organic traffic** shows how well your content draws in visitors on its own. A decrease or unexpected increase in traffic signals a need for a closer look. Was it due to a recent update you made or changes in search engine algorithms? Identifying the cause will help you fine-tune your approach.

Keeping an eye on how your chosen keywords rank in search results is essential for understanding your online visibility. If you're not ranking as well as expected, consider revising your content, adjusting your SEO tactics, or rethinking your keywords.

User behavior metrics are also key indicators of your site's appeal. These metrics, such as the average time spent on your site and the number of pages viewed, offer direct feedback from your audience. They can guide you in making your site more engaging and relevant.

ChatGPT can be an invaluable tool for optimizing your SEO strategies based on analytics and performance data. If analytics show certain content types are more engaging, you can use the AI to produce more of that content efficiently. This way, you'll respond quickly to data-driven insights, enhancing your content strategy.

Practical Tips for SEO Optimization with ChatGPT

An effective SEO strategy involves a holistic approach that aligns with your client's objectives, engages your audience, and adapts to the fast-paced changes in SEO.

Start by thoroughly understanding your **client's goals**. Engage in detailed discussions to grasp what they aim to achieve through SEO, be it boosting organic traffic, enhancing conversion rates, or increasing online visibility. Tailoring your SEO strategies to these goals ensures that your efforts align with your client's vision.

Finding the right keywords is crucial. Identify the ones that are relevant to your client's business and have the potential to drive traffic—keywords that are searched for frequently but aren't too competitive. Once identified, ChatGPT can assist in generating content that incorporates these keywords naturally, is rich in information, and is engaging for readers.

Keep an eye on analytics. Check whether your efforts meet the set **Key Performance Indicators** (KPIs), such as increases in organic traffic or improved engagement metrics. Then, adjust your tactics based on these performance insights.

Be transparent with your clients. Regularly share updates, reports, and actionable insights to keep them in the loop. This helps maintain a trusting relationship and helps you make informed decisions that align with their business goals.

Finally, stay agile. SEO best practices are continually evolving, with algorithms changing frequently. Staying informed about the latest SEO trends and being prepared to change your strategies accordingly is fundamental for staying ahead in the game.

Key Takeaways from Chapter 4

- Craft content that pleases search engines and readers, utilizing ChatGPT to create content rich in relevant keywords and engaging for your audience.

- Organize your content with clear titles, subtitles, and paragraphs. Include links to internal and external pages to improve readability and search engine rankings.

- Tailor your SEO strategies to different types of content. Use ChatGPT to adapt the writing style for blog posts, product descriptions, and landing pages.

- Integrate keywords naturally in your content, starting with the main keyword in the title and introduction and then distributing related keywords throughout the text.

- Keep your content updated with the latest SEO practices and adjust it based on evolving reader interests and SEO trends.

- Conduct in-depth keyword research to understand your audience's language and search terms. For this purpose, tools like SEMrush, Ahrefs, and Google Keyword Planner can give you insights.

- Identify the intent behind searches to create content that matches your audience's needs. This, in turn, improves your content's rankings and user satisfaction.

- Use short-tail and long-tail keywords to balance visibility and competitiveness with the potential for attracting a targeted audience.

- Regularly monitor your SEO strategies' performance with tools like Google Analytics and Google Search Console, adjusting your approach based on real-time data.

- Share regular updates and insights with clients to maintain transparency and make data-driven decisions that align with their SEO goals.

- Stay informed about SEO updates and be willing to adapt your strategies to maintain effectiveness and relevance.

CHAPTER 5: RESUMES AND COVER LETTERS

Drafting Resumes and Cover Letters with ChatGPT

Standout resumes and cover letters are essential for career growth. Each job sector and career level demands a tailored approach to their creation, from the structured chronological resumes common in corporate environments to the skills-oriented functional resumes favored by freelancers. Similarly, cover letters should match the industry's tone, ranging from formal in finance to more creative approaches in marketing fields.

The specificity in your instructions is key to leveraging ChatGPT to draft these important documents. Include detailed guidelines, such as the preferred format and any keywords related to the job or industry, to help ChatGPT produce drafts that meet your specific needs.

The STAR (**Situation, Task, Action, Results**) format is invaluable for developing impactful statements in resumes, effectively showcasing a candidate's achievements and problem-solving skills through concise stories. Guiding ChatGPT to structure accomplishment statements with the STAR method can elevate the narrative, making it more engaging for potential employers.

Example Prompt:

"*I am writing a resume for a candidate applying for a marketing manager position. He needs to update his resume and cover letter to stand out in the competitive field. Given his background as a freelance digital marketing consultant with over five years of experience, I want a resume that highlights his skills and achievements in a format preferred by freelancers and adaptable for corporate positions.*

1. ***Resume:** Write a functional resume emphasizing the candidate's digital*

marketing skills, including SEO, content strategy, and social media marketing. For each key skill, use the STAR format to detail an accomplishment.

2. **Cover Letter:** *Write a cover letter in a creative yet professional tone suitable for a marketing manager role. Highlight the candidate's freelance background as a unique advantage, showcasing adaptability and innovation. Include a brief STAR example, like leading a campaign that significantly improved ROI for a client.*

Ensure the structure is easily customizable for different marketing job applications and effectively showcases the candidate's problem-solving skills and achievements. Ask me questions if you need further details."

While ChatGPT lays down the foundation, infusing each document with your unique insights and understanding of SEO and keyword integration ensures they capture the essence of the candidate's personal brand and stand out to employers. Ultimately, it's your responsibility to adjust the content to reflect the candidate's distinct abilities, experiences, and career goals accurately. This meticulous editing process guarantees that the resume or cover letter is free from errors and truly represents the candidate, enhancing their chances of success in the job market.

Recruitment Landscape and Employer Expectations

In this subchapter, I'll debunk the frequently overlooked aspects of what employers look for and how to align candidate profiles with these expectations.

The **job description** is the first stop, providing insight into the company's culture and values. For instance, a requirement for "*excellent communication skills*" could imply a need for various abilities, ranging from effective written communication to working well in a team setting.

In our digital age, **Applicant Tracking Systems** (ATS) have become the gatekeepers of the recruitment process. These automated systems scan resumes and cover letters for keywords that align with the job role. The challenge is to incorporate these keywords strategically and authentically. Additionally, keeping the document ATS-friendly—meaning free of complex designs and intricate fonts—is essential for passing this initial screening.

Beyond ATS, **Search Engine Optimization** (SEO) has also infiltrated the recruitment landscape. Platforms like LinkedIn function as search engines for recruiters. Optimizing a resume, cover letter, and LinkedIn profile for SEO can significantly increase one's visibility and connect them with potential employers or clients.

Finally, never underestimate the importance of **social proof** in the form of recommendations or endorsements. These elements add another layer of credibility to a candidate's profile, making them more appealing to potential employers. Guide your clients in acquiring targeted LinkedIn recommendations. Encourage them to seek endorsements that underscore specific skills and achievements relevant to their desired job roles.

Maintaining Professionalism and Accuracy

When crafting resumes and cover letters, the importance of precision and professionalism cannot be overstated. These documents carry the weight of your clients' career ambitions, and even a small error could hinder their job prospects. Here are the key principles to ensure your document creation process upholds the highest standards:

Maintain a coherent narrative. Everything from the format and style to its language should work together seamlessly to produce a visually appealing and straightforward document. Use bullet points and choose fonts thoughtfully to enhance readability and structure.

Accuracy is non-negotiable. While tools like grammar and spell-checkers are useful, they're not infallible. A detailed manual review is indispensable. It serves as a final check to catch any mistakes that automated tools might miss, ensuring the documents adhere to the utmost standards of accuracy.

Uphold ethical integrity at all times. Embellishing achievements or altering job titles might be tempting, but maintaining honesty is better. Strive to showcase your clients in the best light without crossing into fabrication, preserving the authenticity of their achievements and experiences.

Customization is key, but it must be rooted in authenticity. Tailor each resume to the job in question, ensuring that all listed skills and experiences are both relevant and verifiable. Strike the right balance between personalization and truthfulness.

Take data privacy seriously. Handling sensitive information requires adherence to strict data privacy laws. Employ secure methods for storing and sharing data, and be transparent with clients about managing their information.

Engage your clients in the process. Involve them in drafting their documents, seeking their input, and ensuring the final version aligns with their career objectives and personal story. This collaborative approach enhances the document's quality while accurately reflecting the client's professional journey.

Allow for revisions and updates. The job search process can evolve, necessitating changes to the documents. Maintain an open dialogue about your working methods, tools, and timelines, encouraging clients to provide new information or adjust their strategy as needed.

By prioritizing professionalism and accuracy in every aspect of document creation, you safeguard your reputation as a trustworthy professional. Moreover, you empower your clients with confidence as they navigate the job market, equipped with impeccable resumes and cover letters that faithfully represent their careers.

Practical Tips for Resumes and Cover Letters Creation

Creating career-defining documents with ChatGPT as your co-author involves a deep dive into the job seeker's world—grasping their career trajectory, skillset, and ambitions.

Tip #1: Understand the distinct roles of resumes and cover letters.

While a resume is a factual recounting of a professional journey, a cover letter offers a personal narrative, tying the job seeker's motivations and aspirations to their professional experiences.

Tip #2: Ensure the documents are optimized for applicant tracking systems (ATS).

This is where ChatGPT comes in handy. It helps embed relevant keywords in a way that balances ATS requirements with engaging content for the human reader. Remember, it's the combination of technology and personal touch that makes the difference.

Tip #3: Pay attention to the refining process.

This phase is all about detail-oriented scrutiny to ensure each word and sentence contributes to a compelling and unified narrative of the job seeker's career. Every job application demands a personalized approach, from subtle language tweaks to significant structural changes, all aimed at resonating with the job and company culture.

Try this exercise to refine your skills with ChatGPT:

Objective: Create a cover letter for a finance professional looking to switch to the tech industry. Begin with ChatGPT to generate a draft, focusing on showcasing transferable skills such as analytical thinking, project management, and collaboration. Highlight the candidate's adaptability and eagerness to learn new technologies. Emphasize how their finance background has honed valuable skills in the tech sector.

Example Prompt:

"Create a cover letter for a finance professional with ten years of experience transitioning to a technology sector role. Focus on highlighting transferable skills such as analytical ability, project management, and teamwork. Emphasize adaptability and eagerness to learn new technologies. Include specific examples of these skills demonstrated in a finance context and how they can be applied in a tech environment. The tone should be professional yet enthusiastic about the career change. Ask me questions if you need more information."

After generating the initial draft with ChatGPT, refine the content to match the individual narrative more closely. This exercise provides insights into crafting documents that effectively speak to career changers, a common scenario in today's job market.

Marketing Resume Services to Job Seekers

Marketing your resume services to job seekers involves understanding and addressing the specific needs of various groups, such as recent graduates, career changers, and experienced executives.

You need to recognize the distinct aspirations and challenges of these groups. Recent graduates might need support in framing their academic achievements as practical, marketable skills. Those contemplating a career shift may seek help highlighting their adaptable skills and navigating a new industry. Executives typically aim to showcase their leadership prowess and strategic impacts.

Highlight your personalized approach and strategic insight in your **value proposition**. Stress the importance of speed, customization, and professionalism. Show potential clients your expertise in crafting resumes and cover letters that genuinely reflect each individual's career journey and goals.

A diverse portfolio showcasing your best work, client success stories, and testimonials can significantly bolster your credibility. To illustrate your effectiveness, focus on the tangible impacts of your services, such as securing interviews or positive feedback from employers.

Leverage content marketing to position yourself as an industry expert. Distributing helpful articles, job search tips, and career advice, especially on platforms like LinkedIn, where your target audience is active, can enhance your visibility and reputation. Aim for educational and relatable content, solidifying your image as a knowledgeable and approachable expert.

Building partnerships with career coaches, recruitment agencies, and educational institutions can also expand your reach. These collaborations can embed your resume services within a broader career support network, offering job seekers a comprehensive package of resources and assistance.

Key Takeaways from Chapter 5

- Standout resumes and cover letters are crucial for career progression. They require customization to fit various job sectors and career levels.

- Provide detailed instructions to ChatGPT, including format preferences and industry-specific keywords, to produce drafts that align with specific needs.

- Utilize the STAR format to develop compelling achievement statements in resumes, guiding ChatGPT to create narratives highlighting problem-solving skills and positive outcomes.

- Refine the AI-generated content to accurately reflect a candidate's unique skills, experiences, and aspirations. Ensure documents are error-free and genuinely represent the individual.

- Align candidate profiles with employer expectations by understanding job descriptions and optimizing for ATS and SEO on platforms like LinkedIn. Highlight social proof through recommendations.

- Maintain professionalism and accuracy in document creation. Ensure coherence, conduct thorough reviews for errors, uphold ethical integrity, and prioritize data privacy.

- Engage clients to ensure documents align with their career goals and personal narratives. Allow for revisions based on feedback or changes in job search strategy.

- Market resume services by understanding the specific needs of target groups. Showcase a personalized approach and use content marketing to establish authority.

- Build partnerships with career coaches, recruitment agencies, and educational institutions to offer comprehensive support to job seekers.

CHAPTER 6: EMAIL MARKETING

Email Content and Newsletters with ChatGPT

Email marketing is about crafting experiences that resonate with your audience and motivate them to engage with your brand. Here's how you can elevate your email content and newsletters using ChatGPT, transforming each message into a powerful engagement tool.

Understand Your Audience Deeply: Begin by examining your audience's preferences, behaviors, and needs. This understanding forms the foundation of your email strategy. When you know what your audience cares about, you can customize your messages to meet them where they are in their journey with your brand.

Crafting a Welcoming First Impression: Your welcome email is the first step in this relationship. It should do more than just say "hello"; it should invite your new subscribers to explore what you offer and encourage them to take their first action with your brand. Use ChatGPT to draft a welcome email that goes beyond the basics, guiding subscribers to your most compelling content or engagingly introducing your product line.

Make Newsletters Must-Read: Turn your regular email updates into eagerly anticipated events. Achieve this by curating content that speaks directly in your brand's voice and resonates with your audience's interests. Provide ChatGPT with your brand messaging and the tone you aim for, and it can help you assemble newsletters that inform and captivate your readers.

Balance in Promotional Emails: When it comes to promotional content, find the sweet spot between highlighting your offers and maintaining a genuine connection with your audience. Imagine crafting an email for a holiday sale infused with a festive spirit, encouraging subscribers to explore your offers in a way that feels like a celebration rather than a sales pitch.

Storytelling That Connects: Stories have a unique power to engage and relate. Whether sharing a customer's success story or the journey behind one of your key products, integrating these narratives into your emails can significantly boost your brand's relatability and memorability. Direct ChatGPT to weave stories that align with your brand values and connect emotionally with your audience.

Elevating Transactional Emails: Even the most routine transactional emails—order confirmations, shipping notices—offer a chance to reinforce your brand voice and deepen customer relationships. Ensure these messages reflect your brand's personality, making every interaction an extension of your brand experience.

By approaching email marketing with a thoughtful and audience-focused strategy and leveraging tools like ChatGPT for content creation, you can develop emails and newsletters that inform, promote, and build lasting connections with your audience.

Email Marketing Strategies and Best Practices

Email marketing is a strategic approach to connecting with your audience effectively. Here's how to refine your email marketing efforts with precision and creativity, leveraging ChatGPT as your tool for success.

Personalization and Segmentation: The era of generic emails is over. Today's consumers expect messages tailored to their specific needs and interests. By analyzing your audience's data, you can segment them into different groups based on their preferences, behaviors, and demographics. Craft messages that cater to the unique needs of each segment. For instance, a promotional email for a new product can be adapted to mirror the interests or past purchases of a particular segment, significantly increasing the chances of engagement and sales.

Crafting Compelling Content: Use ChatGPT to generate content that captivates and educates your readers. Whether it's a dynamic newsletter or an informative blog post, your content should be relevant, engaging, and to the point. Each email should be a stepping stone to build a stronger connection with your subscribers. Incorporate clear calls-to-action (CTAs) that prompt readers to take the desired action, whether that's visiting your site, registering for an event, or making a purchase.

Consistency and Timing: Establishing trust and keeping your audience's attention means staying in regular contact without overwhelming their inboxes. Striking the right balance in your email frequency is key to maintaining interest without becoming intrusive.

Implementing Drip Campaigns and Automation: Leverage these tactics to nurture leads and engage your audience efficiently. Automated email sequences, from welcoming new subscribers to post-purchase follow-ups, offer personalized interactions that can be set up in advance to save time without sacrificing the personalized touch.

Adhering to Best Practices: Beyond timing, frequency and content length are crucial to comply with email regulations like GDPR and CAN-SPAM while maintaining trust and a positive brand image. This includes ethical practices such as regular list cleaning and ensuring an easy unsubscribe process.

Offering Email Marketing Services

With your expertise, creativity, and ChatGPT as your assistant, you're well-equipped to provide email marketing services to all types of businesses, helping them unlock the full potential of their email campaigns.

Identify Your Target Audience: Begin by pinpointing the businesses that could benefit most from your services. This involves understanding the unique challenges and needs of different types of businesses, from small and medium enterprises (SMEs) to e-commerce sites and larger corporations. Tailor your services to meet these specific needs, whether it's driving sales through promotional emails or building a community with newsletters.

Craft Tailored Service Offerings: Your services should span the spectrum of email marketing needs, including campaign strategy development, content creation, and analytics review. Customize these services to address each client's particular objectives, demonstrating your ability to adapt and deliver results across various scenarios.

Strategize and Schedule with Precision: Utilize ChatGPT to generate an initial plan for your email campaigns, incorporating industry insights, target demographics, and key dates. Though ChatGPT's suggestions are a foundation, always refine these plans based on current trends and engagement metrics to ensure maximum effectiveness.

By combining these elements, you'll create a compelling package for businesses aiming to elevate their email marketing efforts. Leverage ChatGPT to streamline content creation, allowing you more time to focus on strategy, data analysis, and fostering client relationships, all key to delivering unparalleled email marketing services.

Analyzing Performance and Optimizing for Conversions

The journey of email marketing doesn't end with hitting "*send.*" Optimizing your email campaigns for better performance and higher conversions is an ongoing process that combines analysis, creativity, and strategic use of AI tools.

Focusing on Key Metrics: The effectiveness of your subject line is the first indicator, acting as the draw to open the email. Once opened, the content must hold attention and lead recipients toward your ultimate aim. The call-to-action (CTA) should be prominently placed and convey urgency or offer value. Experimenting with various CTA designs and locations can help identify what clicks with your audience. Use platforms that provide comprehensive analytics to understand subscriber actions and preferences, enabling informed decisions to refine your campaigns.

The Importance of A/B Testing: Treat A/B testing like a controlled experiment to understand what elements resonate best. By altering one component at a time—be it the subject line, content body, or CTA—on different email versions sent to various audience segments, you can discern which variation performs better. Use ChatGPT as an aid to generate diverse content options for these tests, streamlining the process of creating variations.

Optimizing for Conversions: The ultimate goal of every email element is to drive conversions. This might mean directing traffic to your website, generating leads, or securing sales. Ensure your CTA is visible and compelling enough to encourage the desired action.

By embracing these strategies, you can transform your email marketing efforts into a conversion-generating machine. Remember, the aim is to craft emails that resonate with recipients, prompting them to take action.

Automated Email Responses and Customer Interaction

In the digital age, people expect immediate responses. Therefore, automated email responses become a crucial element of customer service. These automated messages, such as welcome emails, order confirmations, and password resets, often serve as a customer's initial interaction with your brand, setting the stage for your relationship.

Beyond mere greetings or confirmations, the key to making these automated interactions memorable is **personalization**. You need to craft messages that resonate with customer's preferences, activities, or history with your brand. For instance, a welcome email that greets the new subscriber and recommends products or content tailored to their interests can significantly enhance customer engagement.

Here's how to implement this level of personalization using ChatGPT:

Let's take an online bookstore as an example. When a customer signs up for your newsletter indicating an interest in historical fiction, you can create a customized welcome message that reflects this preference. By using ChatGPT, you can develop a template that greets them and recommends books based on their stated preferences. To do so, prompt ChatGPT with specific instructions, such as:

"Generate a welcome email for a new subscriber interested in historical fiction, including three book recommendations and an introduction to our loyalty program."

With details about your loyalty program and the customer's interests, ChatGPT can craft an email that feels personalized and engaging.

Moreover, automated emails should also invite further engagement with your brand. For example, an order confirmation email could offer suggestions for additional products, share information about an upcoming sale, or invite feedback on the purchase experience.

Key Takeaways from Chapter 6

- Crafting engaging emails and newsletters is about creating a meaningful connection with your audience. Tailor each message to spark interest, provide value, and invite action.

- Use ChatGPT to draft welcoming emails that guide new subscribers toward exploring your content or services, making every interaction count right from the start.

- Transform your regular newsletters into eagerly awaited updates by aligning them with your brand's voice and audience's interests.

- When sending out promotional emails, aim for a tone that balances excitement about your offers with the genuine value they provide to your subscribers. The goal is to invite exploration and engagement without overwhelming.

- Incorporating stories into your emails adds a layer of relatability and memorability to your brand. Share successes, journeys, or behind-the-scenes glimpses to build a stronger bond with your audience.

- Don't overlook the importance of transactional emails. Even the most routine communications offer an opportunity to reinforce your brand's voice and deepen the relationship with your customers.

- When offering email marketing services, identify and understand the specific needs of different business types. Then, tailor your offerings to meet those needs effectively.

- Analyzing and optimizing email campaign performance is a continuous process. Utilize key metrics, conduct A/B testing, and constantly refine your approach to ensure your emails resonate with your audience and drive conversions.

- Leveraging ChatGPT for automated email responses can help maintain timely and personalized interaction with customers, enhancing their experience with your brand.

CHAPTER 7: WEBSITE COPYWRITING

Quick Note: I hope you're enjoying the book. If it has resonated with you thus far, your feedback would be invaluable to me. A review on Amazon sharing your experience can greatly support my work and help others discover the book. Your thoughts and reflections are greatly appreciated. You can do so by simply scanning this QR code:

Creating Website Copy with ChatGPT

Creating website copy is basically telling your brand's story online. The pages introduce your brand, describe your products, and share your brand's journey. Each part of your website helps visitors understand what you offer and why it matters to them. Your brand's voice is how you sound to your readers. It's important because it makes your brand unique and recognizable, whether you're aiming to sound serious and professional or friendly and casual.

ChatGPT can help you write all kinds of website content, from product descriptions to blog posts. To get the best results, be clear and specific about what you want. For example, if you're opening an online shop for eco-friendly clothes and want a homepage that appeals to young professionals, you might ask ChatGPT:

"*I'm launching an online store for eco-friendly clothing targeted at young professionals and need compelling homepage copy. The brand voice should be inspiring and approachable, reflecting a blend of professionalism with a friendly tone. This voice should make my brand stand out as unique and recognizable.*

The homepage copy must appeal to young professionals, encouraging them to explore my offerings further.

Write the homepage text covering the following key points:

- *The commitment to eco-friendly and sustainable fashion.*
- *The appeal of my products to the style and conscience of young professionals.*
- *An invitation to explore my product range, emphasizing the impact of their choices on the environment and the fashion industry's future.*

The goal is for visitors to immediately grasp what I offer and why it matters, motivating them to engage with my brand."

The more details you give, the more closely the response will match your needs.

To make your website feel personal and engaging, you can add your own stories or customer reviews to the content ChatGPT creates. This blend of AI efficiency and your personal touch can make your website more relatable and inviting.

To keep your brand's voice consistent across your website, it helps to use a similar style and tone in your prompts to ChatGPT. You can also show it examples of your existing content to help it learn how to match your brand's voice.

The Principles of Effective Web Copywriting

Web copywriting is the art of crafting words that turn website visitors into engaged readers and customers. Here's how to elevate your web copy from good to great:

- **Clear Guidance**: Think of your web copy as a clear guide that leads your readers through your site, from the headline straight to the action you want them to take. It should be obvious to your readers what they should do next, whether that's making a purchase, signing up for more information, or exploring your content further.

- **Conciseness and Richness**: Your copy should get to the point quickly but still be engaging and informative. Like a good espresso, it should give your readers a quick, satisfying taste of your message. Even with longer content, ensure the key points stand out so they're easy for skimmers to grab.

- **Relevance**: Your copy needs to connect with your readers by reflecting both your brand's message and your audience's needs. It's like a conversation where both sides see their reflections in the mirror. Make sure your offerings and messages align with what your audience is looking for.

- **Scannability and SEO**: Good web copy is easy to read and ranks well in search engines. Use clear headings and bullet points, and include keywords naturally to help guide readers and search engines to your content.

- **Emotional Connection**: Lastly, your words should move people. Aim to stir emotions, spark curiosity, or create a sense of urgency. You want to turn passive browsers into active participants who feel connected to your brand.

Following these principles will help transform your web copy from simple text to a powerful tool that engages and motivates your readers.

Offering Web Copywriting Services

Your role is to provide web copywriting services that transform businesses' digital presence. Whether it's a small startup, a bustling e-commerce site, or a comprehensive B2B enterprise, each requires a unique tune that you need to compose.

Understanding Your Audience: Start by diving deep into what different businesses need. A small business might be looking for a captivating copy to make a mark online, while an e-commerce platform needs product descriptions that sell and are also SEO-friendly. B2B companies often look for detailed, authoritative content that speaks to their expertise. Recognizing these varied needs is your first step in tailoring your offerings effectively.

Showcasing Your Portfolio: Think of your portfolio as your showcase, highlighting your versatility and success in achieving key performance indicators such as boosting web traffic, enhancing engagement, or increasing conversions. Include client testimonials, case studies, and specific metrics to provide proof of your impact and establish your credibility.

Flexible Service Offerings: Offer a range of services that meet the diverse needs of your clients. Whether they need compelling home page content, informative blog posts, or a strategic content calendar, make sure you can customize your offerings. This flexibility ensures that every client finds exactly what they're looking for, creating a satisfying and effective partnership.

Pricing Strategy: Your pricing should reflect the quality and value you bring yet be competitive enough to attract a wide range of clients. Be transparent with your pricing, making it clear what clients are getting for their investment. This clarity builds trust and sets the stage for a fruitful collaboration.

By focusing on these aspects, you position yourself as a partner in your client's success, orchestrating web copy that resonates with their audience and achieves their business goals.

Optimizing Web Copy

Transforming your website into a place where visitors feel welcomed and guided towards making a decision is key. Here's how to fine-tune your web copy to boost engagement and drive conversions:

Mapping the User Journey: Think of your web copy as a map for your visitors. From the moment they arrive, you want to lead them smoothly towards making a purchase or taking the desired action. Start by educating them about what you offer as they begin their journey. As they show interest, detailed descriptions and positive feedback from other customers can help them lean closer to a decision. Finally, strong calls-to-action and timely offers can encourage them to take the leap.

Personalization Is Key: Imagine being able to whisper into each visitor's ear, telling them exactly what they need to hear to take the next step. That's the power of personalizing your message. Use data like previous purchases and browsing history to customize your web pages. For an online bookstore, showing book recommendations based on a visitor's past interests can make your site more engaging and increase the likelihood of a sale.

Continual Optimization: Your website is an evolving space. Keeping your web copy fresh and relevant requires ongoing attention. Use tools for SEO analysis and readability checks to ensure your content remains effective and engaging. This means regularly updating your copy to reflect the latest trends, audience preferences, and your brand's goals.

By focusing on these strategies, you create a more engaging and effective website. This approach not only makes the visitor's experience more enjoyable but also increases the likelihood of converting interest into action.

Challenges and Solutions in Web Copywriting

When it comes to copywriting, one of the challenges is the dreaded **writer's block**. Whether it's a lack of inspiration, the burden of perfectionism, or simply mental exhaustion, the key is to keep moving. To combat writer's block, use ChatGPT as a brainstorming partner. When you're stuck, prompt the AI with your topic and ask for various angles or perspectives. If you're writing about sustainable fashion, you could use this prompt:

"*I'm experiencing writer's block while writing an article about sustainable fashion. I'm looking for various angles or perspectives to tackle this topic that provide unique insights for my readers.*

Give me a list of 5 engaging and diverse angles to approach the topic of sustainable fashion. Some areas I'm interested in include:

1. *The environmental impact of traditional vs. sustainable fashion practices.*

> 2. *Innovative materials and technologies driving the sustainable fashion movement.*
>
> 3. *Consumer behavior changes towards sustainability in fashion.*
>
> *My goal is to break through this writer's block by finding a fresh, compelling way to engage with the topic and my audience."*

This approach can provide fresh ideas and reignite your creative spark, helping you overcome the mental block.

Originality is another big challenge. To make sure your web copy is original, input the latest industry trends and key competitor content themes into ChatGPT and ask it to suggest unique content angles. This method can help unearth novel ideas that stand out. ChatGPT's responses will be your foundation for developing trendy and original content.

Remember the importance of **consistency** in brand voice? When refining AI-generated drafts to align with your brand's voice, review the text for tone and style. Compare it to your existing content and adjust the language to match. For instance, if ChatGPT generates a home page description that's too formal, you could rewrite it to be more conversational, or vice versa, depending on your brand's tone. Infuse the copy with brand-specific terms and phrases that resonate with your audience, ensuring the final output is coherent and distinctively "*you*."

Key Takeaways from Chapter 7

- Use ChatGPT to write engaging and informative content across your website, including product descriptions and blog posts.

- Tailor your prompts to be specific to get content that aligns with your brand's voice and audience's interests.

- Effective web copy is clear, concise, relevant, easy to scan, and emotionally engaging. It guides the reader smoothly from introduction to action.

- Understand the unique needs of different businesses, showcase your ability through a versatile portfolio, and offer customizable service packages.

- Clear pricing strategies and demonstrating your ability to improve key performance indicators can help attract clients.

- Map the user journey on your site to guide visitors effectively. Personalize content based on user data to make interactions more relevant.

- Optimize your copy based on SEO and readability to keep your website engaging and effective.

- Overcome writer's block and ensure originality by using ChatGPT as a brainstorming tool to generate fresh content ideas.

- Maintain consistency in your brand's voice by refining AI-generated drafts to align with your brand's tone and style.

CHAPTER 8: PRODUCT DESCRIPTIONS

Crafting Product Descriptions with ChatGPT

Crafting engaging and effective product descriptions for e-commerce means bringing the products to life and making them irresistible to your target audience. Here's how you can use ChatGPT to craft descriptions that enchant and persuade your customers to purchase.

Step 1: The Preparation Stage

When you're getting ready to write a product description, think about how each product fits into your customers' lives and dreams. Your goal is to connect emotionally, showing how the product can enhance their daily routine or fulfill a desire. Whether you're selling the latest tech gadget or a timeless fashion piece, your approach should reflect each item's unique appeal.

Step 2: Creating the Perfect Description with ChatGPT

Gather all the essential details about the product—its features, benefits, and any unique selling points. For example, if you're promoting a vintage-style dress, highlight elements like the fabric's quality, the inspiration behind the design, or how it makes the wearer feel transported to another era. Then, craft a prompt for ChatGPT that includes these details along with the tone and style you're aiming for. If nostalgia and a sense of timeless elegance are what you're going for, make sure to mention that.

Example Prompt:

"I need to create an enticing product description for a vintage-style dress. It's made from high-quality fabric and inspired by 1950s fashion, featuring lace trim and a classic silhouette. I want the description to make

people feel they're stepping back in time, giving a sense of nostalgia and timeless elegance.

Please write a description that:

- *Highlights the dress's quality, design inspiration, and unique details.*
- *Uses a nostalgic and elegant tone.*
- *Appeals to those who love vintage fashion."*

Step 3: Infusing Your Brand's Personality

Every product description should sound like it comes from a unified voice that represents your brand. This consistency helps build trust and loyalty in your customers. If your brand is all about fun and spontaneity, let that shine through in the way you talk about each product. Conversely, if your brand stands for luxury and exclusivity, your descriptions should reflect that sophistication and attention to detail.

Step 4: Connecting with Your Audience

Tailor your product descriptions to speak to your audience's specific interests, needs, and aspirations. Suppose your target market is young professionals looking for eco-friendly fashion choices. In that case, your descriptions should focus on how each piece contributes to a sustainable lifestyle without sacrificing style or professionalism. By aligning your product descriptions with your audience's values and preferences, you increase the relevance of your offerings and the likelihood of conversion.

Each description is an opportunity to tell a story, evoke an emotion, and invite your customer into a world where your product is a must-have. With ChatGPT as your tool and a clear understanding of your products and audience, you're well on your way to creating product descriptions that convert browsers into buyers.

E-commerce Trends and Consumer Behavior

To thrive in the fast-paced world of e-commerce, it is crucial to grasp the market's pulse and consumer preferences. The digital marketplace is an ever-evolving entity shaped by technological advancements, competitive dynamics, and shifting consumer behaviors.

So, how can you create product descriptions that captivate and convert potential buyers?

E-commerce trends shape consumer interaction. Take mobile shopping, for example. Due to the small screen on mobile devices, it's essential that your product descriptions are concise, easily scannable, and have a strong impact. Or consider the growing focus on sustainability. If your product is eco-friendly, it's not just a minor detail but a headline feature that can attract environmentally conscious consumers.

Factors like visual allure, clarity of information, **emotional connection**, and perceived value are the building blocks of your product description. Want to make your listing more effective? Pair high-impact visuals with emotionally resonant copy that speaks to your target audience's dreams and desires.

Trust and **simplicity** are the cornerstones of online purchasing psychology. Your product descriptions should be transparent, highlighting positive reviews or certifications that build trust. Make it easy for the consumer by spelling out the features and benefits clearly and guiding them smoothly to that "*Add to Cart*" button.

Finally, don't forget about SEO. Skillfully integrate keywords to make your product discoverable without making the description read like a jigsaw puzzle.

When leveraging ChatGPT for your product descriptions, feed it with insights from your understanding of e-commerce trends and consumer behavior. This means your prompts should go beyond just product specifications. Give it the context, the mood, and the vibe you want to convey.

Offering Product Description Services

In the crowded digital marketplace, online retailers are in a never-ending race to make their products stand out. Let's find out how to make your services appealing.

Understanding the **specific challenges** and requirements of online retailers is paramount. Whether new entrants or established giants, they all want their products to stand out on the screen. So, product descriptions need to be informative, engaging, and persuasive, all while resonating with the brand's voice and striking the right notes with the target audience.

With ChatGPT in your toolkit, you can offer a scalable, efficient, and customizable content solution. You can write consistent and creative descriptions, adapting to different tones, styles, and product categories. Plus, ChatGPT's efficiency means you can handle the big leagues—retailers with extensive product ranges who need quality and quantity, and they need it fast.

But the journey doesn't end with crafting high-quality descriptions. The nuances of various **e-commerce platforms** must be your area of expertise. Each platform has its audience and style. For example, on Amazon, your focus might be on detailed specifications and bullet points for a clear, concise presentation. On Etsy, however, you might want something that resonates with a community that values creativity and personal touch. Imagine a handmade ceramic vase: on Amazon, you'll need to highlight its dimensions, durability, and functional aspects, while on Etsy, you'll tell a story about its artisanal creation and unique design elements.

Effective **client communication** is pivotal in gathering information for compelling product descriptions. Start by asking detailed questions about the product, including its features, benefits, target audience, and what sets it apart in the market. Also, inquire about the client's brand voice and any specific messaging they wish to convey. This approach demonstrates your commitment to aligning with the client's overall marketing strategy, building trust, and ensuring client satisfaction.

Optimizing Product Descriptions

Optimizing product descriptions for conversions and SEO is a must in the e-commerce world, where every click counts, and consumer attention is a valuable commodity.

Imagine your product description as a shop in a bustling marketplace. SEO is the signboard that makes people stop and look. It all comes down to strategically placing keywords where they will have the most significant impact. Tools like SEMrush and Google Keyword

Planner will be essential in this game. They direct you to relevant keywords with high buying intent.

But here's where many people go wrong: SEO isn't the endgame; it's the opening act. What keeps a potential customer interested after they click through? Your product description takes center stage at this point, functioning as both an informative guide and a persuasive salesperson. As discussed in Chapter 4, the key is seamlessly blending keywords into these descriptions.

Conversions are driven by copy that resonates. Listing features is not enough; you need to translate them into benefits. Don't just say that the smartphone has a "*long-lasting battery*"; tell them they can "*binge-watch their favorite shows all day without a recharge.*" And always make a clear call to action.

Finally, don't forget mobile users, who often browse on smaller screens in shorter time frames. Your descriptions should be mobile-friendly. Think bullet points, concise sentences, and high-quality images that serve as a visual aid to your textual content.

Practical Tips for Product Description Writing with ChatGPT

While the previous chapters laid the foundation for using ChatGPT in writing different types of content, I will now introduce some advanced techniques that can further enhance your craft.

A key advanced feature of ChatGPT-4 is its ability to modulate tone and incorporate **emotive language**, which can significantly impact the effectiveness of a product description. For instance, when creating a description for luxury skincare products, a prompt like:

"*Write a 100-word product description for a luxury skincare cream, using a tone of sophistication and elegance and emphasizing the feeling of indulgence it provides*" leverages ChatGPT's strengths. Such targeted prompts ensure that the output aligns seamlessly with your client's brand voice, engaging the target audience emotionally.

Understanding **consumer psychology** is crucial for creating compelling product descriptions. You could use ChatGPT to craft descriptions that create a sense of urgency or exclusivity, common psychological triggers that drive conversions. For example, a prompt like:

"*Write a description for a limited-edition sneaker, highlighting its exclusivity and the urgency to purchase before it sells out*" can yield a description that informs and motivates the consumer to act promptly.

And why not use ChatGPT for **keyword research** as well? Input the product type into the AI, like "*eco-friendly yoga mats*," and ask it to generate a list of relevant, search-engine-friendly keywords. Need to outshine the competition? Ask ChatGPT to summarize key features found in competitors' descriptions. This data becomes your secret weapon in crafting descriptions that stand out and speak directly to the market.

Embrace this journey as a continuous learning curve. Experiment with different prompts and styles, and always be open to adapting your methods. Remember, the goal is to describe a product and bring it to life in the consumer's mind, creating a vivid picture that motivates purchase decisions.

Key Takeaways from Chapter 8

- Before writing, gather all the facts about your product—its features, the problems it solves, and why it's better than others.

- Equally important is understanding who you're selling to. What does your ideal customer care about?

- Armed with product insights and customer understanding, guide ChatGPT with detailed prompts to generate descriptions that resonate.

- Your product descriptions should echo your brand's voice. If your brand is playful and quirky, let that shine through in how you describe each item. This consistency reinforces your brand identity and fosters a stronger connection with your audience.

- Beyond the basics of the product, weave stories into your descriptions. How did this product come to be? Is there a particular problem it was created to solve? Stories engage the emotional side of your customers, making the product more memorable and desirable.

- Tailor your descriptions to speak directly to the needs and desires of your audience. Highlight how your product fits into their lifestyle or solves a specific problem they face.
- ChatGPT can help you explore various angles to present your product in the light most likely to convert browsers into buyers.

CHAPTER 9: TRAVEL BLOGS AND GUIDES

Creating Content for Travel Blogs with ChatGPT

It's Monday morning, and you're sitting at your desk, yearning to escape the daily grind. You open up a travel blog, and suddenly, you're transported to the sun-drenched beaches of Bali or the bustling streets of Tokyo. That's the power of compelling travel content. But how do you write stories that inform and inspire?

Whether you're writing about the thrill of skydiving in New Zealand or the peaceful solitude of a Himalayan retreat, ChatGPT can help you draft content that hits the right notes. Feed it the right prompts, and you'll have a draft covering everything from the must-see landmarks to those hidden gems only locals know about. Then, your personal experiences and insights will make that content truly unforgettable.

But to make your content stand out as authentic, you need to strike that delicate balance between informative and relatable. Whether you're catering to budget backpackers or luxury seekers, AI can tailor your content to speak directly to the reader's experiences and aspirations. It's about crafting narratives that readers can see themselves in.

For instance, when targeting budget travelers, you might prompt ChatGPT to focus on affordable accommodations and free attractions, while luxury travelers would appreciate content on upscale experiences and exclusive venues. Adjusting your prompts accordingly lets you get nuanced narratives that resonate with each unique group.

Example Prompt:

"Generate a detailed 1000-word draft for a travel blog post about budget-friendly exploration in Tokyo, Japan. Include sections on affordable accommodations, free or low-

cost landmarks and attractions, and hidden gems. The post should be engaging, offering readers a vivid picture of experiencing Tokyo, and provide practical tips for navigating the city on a budget."

Travel Trends and Audience Preferences

Expert travel blogging requires a keen understanding of both current travel trends and your audience's specific interests. Here's how to craft content that resonates deeply and engages your readers:

Stay Updated on Travel Trends: Your blog should guide readers through the latest in travel. Whether it's the increasing interest in eco-tourism, the convenience of city passes, or the charm of hidden local spots, aligning your content with these trends provides value and positions your blog as an authoritative source in the travel community.

Explore Diverse Themes: Don't hesitate to explore various topics. From the practicalities of travel insurance for globe-trotters to the allure of under-the-radar destinations, variety enriches your blog. Consider sections dedicated to sustainable travel, cultural exploration, or tips for digital nomads. Catering to various interests broadens your audience and keeps your content dynamic and engaging.

Understand Your Audience: Who reads your blog? Identify your audience segments—families looking for kid-friendly vacations, solo travelers searching for adventure, or couples seeking romantic getaways. Tailor your content to meet these diverse needs. Share insights on the best family resorts, top adventure destinations for solo travelers, or the most romantic retreats. Personalizing your content in this way ensures it speaks directly to your readers' desires.

Incorporate Personal Insights and Stories: What truly distinguishes your blog is your personal touch. Share your adventures, the lessons you've learned, and the people you've met. These stories enhance your content's authenticity and build a deeper connection with your audience.

By combining an understanding of the latest travel trends with a deep dive into your audience's preferences and peppering your content with personal anecdotes, your travel blog can become a go-to resource for travelers seeking inspiration, advice, and a sense of community. It's your unique perspective and insights that will make your blog pop out in the vast sea of travel content online.

Diversifying Content to Cover Various Travel Destinations

To make your travel blog a vibrant and inclusive platform, it's essential to diversify your content to appeal to a broad spectrum of travelers. Here are my top tips:

Cover a Wide Range of Destinations: Your blog should showcase everything from bustling city escapes to serene countryside retreats. Consider including destinations catering to various interests and budgets, ensuring every reader finds something that sparks their wanderlust.

Tailor Content to Different Traveler Types: Recognize the diversity within your audience.

Some readers may seek adventure and exploration, while others might prefer relaxation or cultural immersion. Develop content segments specifically for families, solo travelers, couples, or groups with different interests, such as eco-tourism, food tourism, or historical tours.

Interactive Elements: Enhance your blog with interactive features like travel maps or quizzes. For instance, create a map highlighting off-the-beaten-path destinations or a quiz that helps readers discover their next travel spot based on their preferences. These tools engage readers more deeply with your content and provide them with personalized value.

Promote Ethical and Sustainable Travel: Encouraging responsible travel practices is crucial. Include tips on respecting local cultures, minimizing environmental impact, and supporting local economies. Educating your readers about these practices not only enriches their travel experience but also contributes to a more sustainable and ethical tourism industry.

Utilize ChatGPT for Research and Ideas: Leverage ChatGPT to generate ideas for covering new destinations or travel trends. Ask it to suggest content addressing specific traveler needs or emerging interests. This can help you keep your blog fresh and relevant.

By incorporating these strategies, you'll create a travel blog that serves as a comprehensive guide for a diverse audience. Whether your readers seek adventure, relaxation, cultural experiences, or sustainable travel options, they'll find valuable insights and inspiration on your platform. Your goal is to create a space where every reader can find their next dream destination and feel equipped and inspired to explore the world responsibly and joyfully.

Ensuring Accuracy in Travel Content

Your mission is to be a reliable guide for your readers, ensuring that the information you provide is accurate and ethical. Here are some strategies to enhance the reliability and integrity of your travel blog:

Maintain Up-to-Date Information: The travel landscape is ever-changing, with new regulations, closures, and attractions updating frequently. Dedicate time to reviewing and updating your posts regularly to reflect the latest conditions. This might involve checking official tourism sites or utilizing real-time data sources to verify information.

Promote Cultural Sensitivity and Environmental Responsibility: Be mindful of the impact your recommendations can have on destinations and communities. Aim to educate your readers about local customs and traditions, encouraging respectful and responsible tourism. Highlight eco-friendly practices and businesses that contribute positively to their local environments and communities.

Respond Quickly to Global Changes: The world can change rapidly, affecting travel plans and safety. Develop a system to quickly incorporate significant global events into your content. This might include updating travel advisories, providing resources for impacted travelers, or even pausing content promotion in light of sensitive situations.

Fact-Check and Verify: Leverage reliable sources to confirm the details you share. While ChatGPT-4 offers internet browsing capabilities, always cross-reference this information with official and up-to-date sources like government websites, reputable news outlets, and direct communications with local authorities or businesses.

Ethical Storytelling: When sharing travel stories or highlighting destinations, consider the narrative you're contributing to. Ensure that your content doesn't inadvertently exploit or misrepresent cultures and communities. Strive for stories that celebrate diversity and foster understanding.

By adhering to these principles, you solidify your travel blog as a trusted resource for insightful, respectful, and current travel information. Your readers will value the care you take in guiding them, ensuring that their adventures are informed, ethical, and enriching.

Practical Tips for Travel Content Creation with ChatGPT

The cornerstone of any great travel story is an in-depth understanding of the destination. Before you even begin to write, you must immerse yourself in the culture, history, and unique offerings of the place you'll cover. For instance, if you're writing about Kyoto, Japan, ask ChatGPT to provide information on Kyoto's cultural heritage, popular tourist spots, and hidden gems. You might use a prompt like:

"*I'm writing a travel blog post about Kyoto, Japan, and I need to explore what makes the city special. I want to cover Kyoto's cultural heritage, well-known tourist attractions, and some hidden gems that aren't as famous but incredibly captivating.*

Please give me detailed information on:

- *Kyoto's cultural heritage and history.*
- *Popular tourist spots in Kyoto.*
- *Hidden gems or less-known places in Kyoto worth visiting.*

I aim to give readers a comprehensive view of Kyoto, mixing well-known sights with the city's secret spots, all steeped in rich culture and history."

Move beyond the commonplace formats saturating the web. Readers yearn for fresh perspectives and novel insights. Leverage ChatGPT also as a collaborator in brainstorming creative content angles. This could mean shifting focus from typical tourist guides to immersive storytelling that captures the essence of a destination.

The world of travel is fluid, constantly reshaped by global developments, emerging trends, and evolving traveler preferences. Your content should reflect this dynamism. Continuously update your knowledge and adapt your writing to remain relevant and resonant with your audience. This means revisiting destinations in your content with new angles, responding to the latest travel norms, and predicting future trends.

Key Takeaways from Chapter 9

- Utilize ChatGPT to draft initial content that covers must-see landmarks, hidden gems, and personal insights to make travel stories engaging and unforgettable.

- Customize your travel content to match the experiences and aspirations of your target audience.

- Align your content with current travel trends and interests to keep your blog relevant. This will position your platform as an authoritative source in the travel community.

- Explore various topics, destinations, and experiences to cater to your audience's interests, enriching your blog with diverse and engaging content.

- Identify distinct segments within your audience and tailor your content to meet their specific travel needs and preferences, enhancing personalization.

- Share your personal travel experiences, insights, and lessons learned to add authenticity to your content and foster a deeper connection with your readers.

- Update your posts regularly to reflect the latest information and maintain the factual integrity of your content, building trust with your readers.

- Craft content that respects the cultures and communities you write about, encouraging responsible and ethical travel practices among your readers.

- Experiment with ChatGPT to generate unique content ideas, break conventional blogging formats, and continuously adapt your content strategy to the evolving travel landscape.

CHAPTER 10: SCRIPT WRITING

Drafting Scripts with ChatGPT

Whether you're scripting for videos, podcasts, or advertisements, the essence of scriptwriting remains the same—it's about telling a story that captures and holds your audience's attention.

For videos, the script lays the groundwork for what the audience sees and hears. It's not only the words spoken by the characters or narrators but also setting the scene visually and audibly. A video script for YouTube should describe the setting, suggest camera angles, and even recommend types of background music or sound effects to enhance the storytelling.

When it comes to podcasts, the script is primarily focused on what is heard. Since there are no visual cues, the script must be detailed in its descriptions and clear in its narrative structure. The language should be engaging and paced to keep listeners hooked, with enough variation in tone and subject matter to maintain interest throughout the episode.

For advertisements, the script must be concise and impactful. With only a short time to grab the audience's attention and convey a message, every word counts. The script should quickly establish a connection with the viewer or listener, present a problem or need, offer a solution, and call to action—all within a few seconds.

ChatGPT can be a valuable tool in crafting scripts across these different formats. To make the most of ChatGPT for scriptwriting, try the following:

1. **Be clear about the format and purpose**: Specify the type of script you're working on (video, podcast, advertisement) and its objective.

2. **Provide detailed instructions**: Include information about your target audience, the script's tone (informative, humorous, emotional), and any key

messages or calls to action that need to be included.

3. **Use iterations**: Don't hesitate to refine your prompts based on the outputs you receive. ChatGPT can generate various versions of your script, allowing you to explore different approaches and refine your narrative.

Example Prompt:

"*I'm working on a script for a YouTube video titled 'The Hidden Gems of Tokyo: A Travel Guide.' The goal is to engage viewers by exploring unique, less-known attractions in Tokyo, offering a fresh perspective on travel in the city.*

Format and Purpose: a script for a YouTube video focusing on Tokyo's hidden gems.

Length: a script that would result in a 5-minute video.

Target Audience: Young adults and seasoned travelers seeking unique, authentic travel experiences.

Tone of the Script: Engaging and informative, with a light-hearted, adventurous tone to maintain viewer interest and entertainment.

Key Elements to Include*:*

- ***Opening Scene****: A vivid introduction to Tokyo, emphasizing the city's blend of bustling urban life and hidden serene spots.*

- ***Visual and Audible Suggestions****: Include camera shots of less-known locales, suggesting upbeat background music to match the excitement of discovery.*

- ***Narrative Structure****: For each hidden gem, provide a short backstory or unique details, highlighting what makes these places special.*

- ***Closing****: Conclude with a summary of the adventures and encourage viewers to explore Tokyo's less-trodden paths. Include a call to action for viewers to like, share, and subscribe for more guides.*

Draft a script incorporating these specifications, ensuring the content fits the 5-minute video format and effectively guides viewers through Tokyo's hidden attractions. Ask me questions if you need more information."

Scriptwriting software like Final Draft and Celtx can help format your script according to industry standards. However, the essence of a great script comes from understanding your medium and audience. Combine this understanding with ChatGPT's capabilities, and you have the potential to create scripts that truly resonate with your viewers or listeners.

Scriptwriting for Different Platforms

Scriptwriting varies significantly across different platforms, each with its own requirements and audience expectations. For YouTube videos, scripts need to be visually driven and incorporate relevant keywords to perform well in search algorithms. It's important to write in an engaging way that keeps viewers interested. Also, consider accessibility by ensuring your script translates well into closed captions.

In podcasting, the script is everything. Since there's no visual element, your words must paint the picture. Use sound effects judiciously to add layers to your narrative, play with voice modulation to enhance storytelling, and utilize pauses effectively to give listeners time to think and feel. Your script should flow like a natural conversation but carry the weight of a well-told story.

Television scripts combine visual and auditory storytelling, requiring a keen balance of dialogue, visual cues, and action. They must also fit within specific time constraints and accommodate commercial breaks, making pacing crucial. Writing for television involves deeply understanding the visual medium and anticipating how scenes unfold on screen.

Understanding your audience is important regardless of the platform. A script that engages a younger YouTube audience might not resonate on a podcast targeting professionals. Tailor your language, style, and content to match your audience's preferences and interests to maximize engagement and impact.

Creativity and Originality in Scriptwriting

When you're working on a script, creativity and originality are key. ChatGPT can give you many ideas to start with, but the real magic happens when you add your personal touch to those ideas. Here's a detailed approach to making your scripts stand out.

1. **Leverage AI for Preliminary Drafts**: Begin by using ChatGPT to generate foundational elements of your script. This could include basic dialogue between characters, plot outlines, or thematic concepts.

2. **Infuse Depth and Complexity**: Examine the AI-generated draft through a creative lens. Look for opportunities to add depth to your characters and complexity to your plot. This might involve exploring a character's backstory, motivations, or internal conflicts in greater detail or perhaps introducing nuanced plot developments that add layers of intrigue and engagement.

3. **Refine Dialogue for Authenticity**: Dialogues are the lifeblood of any script, conveying the essence of characters and advancing the plot. Take the dialogues suggested by AI and refine them to ensure they authentically reflect the characters' personalities and the script's tone. Consider the nuances of language, dialect, and speech patterns that make each character unique.

4. **Introduce Creative Twists and Turns**: Use your imagination to enhance the plot with unexpected twists, emotional depth, or thematic richness that AI might not have originally included. This could mean weaving in a surprising plot twist that challenges the characters (and audience) or deepening the thematic exploration to add layers of meaning.

5. **Polish with Detail and Texture**: The devil is in the details. Enrich your script with vivid descriptions of settings, precise character details, and atmospheric elements that bring your narrative world to life. These details enhance visual

imagination and ground your story in a tangible reality.

6. **Ensure Originality and Freshness**: During the creative process, constantly evaluate your script for originality. Your goal is to present narratives and characters that stand out for their uniqueness and authenticity. Your creative vision will ensure your script offers your audience a fresh and engaging experience.

7. **Break Through Creative Blocks**: Should you encounter writer's block, you can count on ChatGPT as a source of creative stimulation. Challenge the AI with prompts that push the boundaries of your narrative, explore genres or themes outside your comfort zone, or even ask it to generate the most bizarre plot twists. These exercises can invigorate your creativity, providing new pathways for exploration.

8. **Iterate and Evolve**: Scriptwriting is inherently iterative. Use ChatGPT's feedback loop to refine and evolve your script continuously. Each iteration should aim to heighten emotional

impact, sharpen narrative focus, and enhance the overall storytelling experience.

By following this detailed approach, leveraging both AI's capabilities and your unique creative flair, you can craft scripts that are original, engaging, and deeply resonant with your audiences. The alchemy of scriptwriting lies in transforming the ordinary into the extraordinary, a task that demands both innovative technology and the irreplaceable human touch.

Practical Tips for Scriptwriting with ChatGPT

Remember we said that even the most advanced AI requires a human touch to shine? In this section, we'll look at how we can make this collaboration a success.

Your prompts are your most powerful weapon. The more specific your genre, tone, and key plot elements are, the better the AI will perform.

Providing ChatGPT with the backstory, character arcs, and settings enables it to generate dialogues and scenarios that flow naturally into your story, ensuring each piece fits into the larger picture.

Try the following exercise to hone your prompt-crafting skills:

Take a basic plot idea, such as a romantic comedy about two chefs in a competitive cooking show. Now, experiment with these prompts:

1. *"Write a dialogue between two rival chefs who fall in love, keeping the tone light and humorous."*

2. *"Suggest three plot twists for a romantic comedy set in a cooking show, where the main characters are rival chefs."*

Observe how small changes in your prompts can lead to significantly different AI-generated content. This exercise will help you understand the importance of specificity and clarity in your prompts. Feel free to experiment with other prompts, adding different details each time to see what happens.

Consistency is the glue that holds your script together. Whether it's keeping the tone consistent or making sure the characters follow their storylines, it is essential. Your screenplay's framework is its structure. Those ideas need a framework—a clear beginning, a tension-filled middle, and a satisfying conclusion. Your job is to arrange every "note" so the story flows smoothly.

Characters are the soul of your script. As the story progresses, they must evolve, grow, and change. Ensure their actions and dialogues are consistent and meaningful, adding to the story in an engaging and believable way. Remember that your script needs to be respectful and inclusive. So, use plagiarism checkers, like Turnitin or Copyscape, to add the finishing touches.

Key Takeaways from Chapter 10

- Use ChatGPT for foundational script elements. Start by generating basic dialogues, plot outlines, or themes.

- Enhance AI drafts by adding emotional depth to characters and refining the dialogue to ensure it's true to each character's voice.

- Introduce unexpected twists or enriching details to make the script more captivating and original.

- Ensure your script has unique narratives and characters, avoiding clichés and generic plots.

- Employ ChatGPT to brainstorm and overcome writer's block by generating diverse ideas and dialogues.

- Embrace the iterative nature of scriptwriting, using feedback to improve and evolve your script.

- Crafting precise and detailed prompts can significantly enhance the relevance and quality of AI-generated content.

- Ensure your script maintains a consistent tone and follows a coherent structure from start to finish.

- Characters should grow, and their actions and dialogues should contribute meaningfully to the story.

- Be mindful of inclusivity and cultural sensitivity in your writing.

- Use tools like Turnitin or Copyscape to ensure your script is plagiarism-free.

CHAPTER 11: AD COPYWRITING

Drafting Ad Copies with ChatGPT

Drafting persuasive ad copies with ChatGPT means combining your brand's unique appeal with the tool's capability to generate targeted messages. The process is about crafting a message that represents your audience and showcases your brand effectively. For example, when creating an ad for a fitness app, detail the app's features and your audience's needs in your prompt to ChatGPT.

Incorporating ChatGPT into your wider marketing strategy, alongside other digital tools, enhances the cohesion and effectiveness of your campaigns. For instance, in a social media campaign for a new fashion line, you could use ChatGPT for initial drafts and refine your messaging based on analytics from social media tools. This integration allows for message optimization based on audience response, improving the campaign performance.

Monitoring **key metrics** like engagement rate, click-through rate (CTR), and conversion rate is crucial in evaluating the success of your ad campaigns. These metrics offer insights into how well your ad resonates with the audience, the effectiveness of your call to action, and the overall impact of your ad in driving conversions.

This chapter will guide you through the nuances of ad copywriting, combining advertising fundamentals with consumer psychology insights to create compelling ad copies. You'll learn how to utilize ChatGPT's capabilities to produce ad content that engages and converts while positioning you as a skilled professional in the industry.

Advertising Principles and Consumer Psychology

Understanding the foundational principles of advertising and consumer psychology is crucial for creating ads that connect and resonate with your audience. The core elements of effective advertising can be distilled into clarity, relevance, uniqueness, and a compelling call to action.

- **Clarity** means delivering your message in a straightforward manner, ensuring your audience understands what you're offering without any confusion.

- **Relevance** ensures your ad speaks directly to your target audience's interests and needs, making them feel seen and understood.

- **Uniqueness** distinguishes your ad from competitors, highlighting what makes your brand or product special.

- **A compelling call to action** encourages your audience to take the next step, whether it's making a purchase, subscribing to a newsletter, or following your brand on social media.

Incorporating insights from consumer psychology can significantly enhance the impact of your ads. Psychological triggers such as reciprocity, commitment, and social proof play pivotal roles in influencing consumer behavior. By understanding and ethically leveraging these triggers, you can craft ads that capture attention and motivate action.

Additionally, it's important to consider the consumer journey, recognizing that different messages may be required at various stages. Tailoring your ad copy to address your audience's specific needs and motivations at each point in their journey can lead to higher engagement and conversion rates.

ChatGPT can be an invaluable tool in this process, acting as a resource for generating ad copy that effectively combines these advertising principles with psychological insights. By inputting detailed information about your target audience and marketing goals, ChatGPT can help you create ad messages that are both compelling and resonant.

Example Prompt:

"*I'm creating an Instagram post ad for my newest eco-friendly skincare line, targeting environmentally conscious consumers aged*

20-30. They value the quality of their skincare and the ethical and environmental impact of the products they choose. My products are made from 100% natural ingredients, are cruelty-free, and are packaged in fully recyclable materials, aligning with my audience's values.

Ad Details:

- **Length**: *The ad should be concise, about 50 words, ideal for Instagram.*

- **Clarity**: *communicate my skincare line's eco-friendly attributes clearly and succinctly.*

- **Relevance**: *speak directly to my eco-conscious audience, emphasizing sustainability and ethical responsibility.*

- **Uniqueness**: *My brand's unique selling point is a commitment to the environment— I pledge to plant a tree for each product sold. This should be a focal point in the ad.*

- **Compelling Call to Action**: *motivate the audience to visit my website to learn more about my products and receive a discount on their first purchase.*

Incorporate Psychological Triggers:

- *Use the principle of **reciprocity** by highlighting my tree-planting initiative and suggesting that purchasing from me contributes to global reforestation efforts.*

- *Create a sense of **community and commitment** by inviting viewers to join my movement towards more sustainable living through their skincare choices.*

Write an ad that encapsulates these elements, with a message that resonates deeply with the target audience's desire to make positive environmental choices without compromising on the quality of their skincare regimen."

Offering Ad Copywriting Services

Offering ad copywriting services involves strategy, marketing, and understanding the needs and challenges of your potential clients.

Here's how you can turn your ability to craft compelling ad copy into a successful business:

1. **Identify Your Target Clients**: Your clients could be anyone from small local businesses to large corporations, each with unique needs. For example, a small café might need help creating an ad about their morning coffee that evokes the cozy, welcoming atmosphere of their establishment. Your job is to transform simple messages into captivating narratives that appeal to the target audience.

2. **Develop a Range of Services**: Leverage ChatGPT to offer a variety of services, such as creating multiple ad versions for A/B testing or tailoring messages for different audience segments. This approach allows you to provide comprehensive solutions that go beyond basic copywriting, including performance analysis and iterative improvements.

3. **Market Your Services Creatively**: Use various platforms to market your services. Instagram and LinkedIn can be powerful tools for showcasing your

work and sharing industry insights. Consider starting a blog where you offer copywriting tips and discuss trends, utilizing ChatGPT to generate content. Being active on the platforms where your potential clients spend their time increases your visibility and establishes your expertise.

4. **Maintain Clear Communication with Clients**: Clear and consistent communication is essential once you start working with clients. Set expectations regarding timelines and deliverables from the outset. Regular updates and open lines of communication build trust and facilitate collaboration.

5. **View Feedback as an Opportunity**: Feedback is invaluable for refining your work and better understanding your client's needs. If a client feels that their brand's essence isn't fully captured, use it as an opportunity to delve deeper into their vision. Engaging in detailed discussions about their brand and expectations can help you craft copy that truly resonates, strengthening your

relationship and positioning you as a trusted partner.

The key to success lies in understanding your client's unique challenges, providing tailored solutions, and building strong, communicative relationships.

Optimizing Ad Copy for Conversion

Optimizing ad copy is crucial for converting readers into customers and engaging them with your brand. It's about ensuring every word aligns with the brand's voice and meets the audience's needs. Here's how you can do just that:

1. **Harmonize with Your Brand and Audience**: Your ad copy should reflect the brand's voice and speak directly to the audience's preferences and needs. Like music notes in a symphony, every word in your ad copy must work together to produce a cohesive message that resonates with your audience.

2. **Use ChatGPT for Data-Driven Insights**: Leverage ChatGPT to incorporate words and phrases proven to engage and convert. By analyzing performance data, ChatGPT can help tailor your ad copy to include elements that have historically driven conversions and engagement.

3. **Guide the Audience to Action**: Your ad copy should also inspire action. From raising awareness to sparking interest and ultimately leading to conversion, your copy should guide the audience through this journey. Strategic word placement is key to attracting attention and motivating action.

4. **Measure Success with Metrics**: Utilize metrics such as click-through rate, conversion rate, and engagement rate to gauge the effectiveness of your ad copy. These numbers will tell you what works and what doesn't, allowing for continual optimization.

By following these steps and using ChatGPT strategically, you can create ad copy that engages your audience and drives them to action. This process of continuous optimization, informed by data and creative insight, will help you achieve better results with your advertising efforts.

Practical Tips for Ad Copywriting with ChatGPT

When creating ad copies, it's important to craft messages that capture attention and drive conversions. Here are five practical tips for achieving this with ChatGPT:

Tip #1: Understand Your Offering.

Start by thoroughly understanding what you are advertising. Identify what makes your product or service unique and how it solves your consumers' problems or meets their needs. Knowing your unique selling propositions (USPs) allows you to articulate them well in compelling narratives, highlighting your audience's value.

Tip #2: Use Strategic Creativity.

Apply creativity with a strategic approach. For instance, instead of a generic ad copy, use a detailed prompt that encompasses the product's benefits and aligns with your brand values, like sustainability for an organic skincare line. This method produces ad copies that resonate more effectively with your target audience by integrating the product's benefits with broader themes, such as environmental responsibility.

Tip #3: Leverage SEO.

Incorporate SEO principles to ensure your ad copy is visible to your target audience. Use relevant keywords your potential customers are likely searching for. This increases the chances of your ad appearing in search results, thereby improving visibility and engagement.

Tip #4: Experiment with A/B Testing.

Utilize A/B testing to compare different versions of your ad copy. This involves changing elements such as the headline, call to action, or messaging to see which variant performs better. A/B testing is invaluable for optimizing your ad copies based on real audience responses, allowing you to refine your message for maximum impact.

Tip #5: Incorporate Feedback.

Use insights gained from SEO and A/B testing to continuously refine your ad copy. Feedback from these tests can guide how you adjust your messaging, tone, and even the strategic focus of your ads to better connect with your audience.

The goal is to blend creativity with strategy, using data-driven insights to craft messages that appeal to and compel your audience to act.

Key Takeaways from Chapter 11

- Utilize ChatGPT to create ad copies that resonate with your brand's unique features and your target audience's needs.

- Combine ChatGPT's capabilities with other digital tools to enhance the cohesion and effectiveness of marketing campaigns.

- Keep an eye on the engagement rate, click-through rate (CTR), and conversion rate to gauge the success of your ad campaigns. These metrics provide insights into the resonance of your message, the effectiveness of your call to action, and the impact of your ad in driving conversions.

- Master the core elements of effective advertising—clarity, relevance, uniqueness, and a compelling call to action.

- Incorporate consumer psychology insights, such as reciprocity, commitment, and social proof, to enhance the persuasiveness of your ads.

- Identify your target clients across various industries and tailor your services to their specific needs.

- Develop a versatile portfolio, communicate your process, and market your services using platforms where your potential clients are active.

- Harmonize your ad copy with the brand's voice and audience's needs, leveraging ChatGPT for data-driven insights.

- Understand your product/service, use strategic creativity, incorporate SEO principles, and experiment with A/B testing.

- Continuously refine your ad copy based on feedback to create compelling messages that drive conversions.

CHAPTER 12: SOCIAL MEDIA MANAGEMENT

ChatGPT for Social Media Content Creation

In the evolving social media landscape, brands constantly seek innovative ways to capture their audience's attention. With the introduction of AI tools like ChatGPT, creating content that resonates with viewers has become more accessible and efficient.

The key to a successful social media strategy lies in understanding the importance of a **content calendar**. This tool is a strategic plan that ensures your brand consistently engages with its audience, offering them value at every touchpoint.

Furthermore, maintaining a distinct and resonant **brand voice** across all platforms is crucial. It's what makes a brand memorable and builds a connection with the audience. ChatGPT can help amplify this brand voice, ensuring that every post, tweet, or story feels authentic and aligned with the brand's essence.

Analytics are also very important in this digital strategy. By integrating analytics tools, you can gauge the effectiveness of your content in real-time, allowing for agile adjustments that can significantly enhance engagement rates and ROI. This data-driven approach ensures that your strategies are based on actual performance metrics.

This chapter will provide a comprehensive look at effectively using ChatGPT for social media content creation. From developing a content calendar that tells your brand's story to employing analytics for strategy refinement, the insights and strategies outlined here are designed to elevate your social media management and ensure your brand pops out in the digital crowd.

Maintaining a Consistent Brand Voice

Your unique voice is what differentiates your brand, making it memorable and engaging for your audience. With ChatGPT, you have a tool at your disposal to consistently articulate this voice, whether it's through social media posts, customer service interactions, or content marketing.

The first step to effectively using ChatGPT for this purpose is to establish a detailed **brand guideline**. This document should outline the nuances of your brand's voice, including its tone, language, and any phrases or terminology that are essentially "*you*." These guidelines direct ChatGPT to communicate in a way that's true to your brand's identity.

To ensure ChatGPT accurately reflects your brand's voice, it's essential to fine-tune it with specific examples that exemplify your unique style. If your brand's voice is characterized by humor and informality, provide ChatGPT with examples of past content that showcases these traits. Updating the AI with fresh examples and trends will keep your brand's voice relevant and relatable, enabling it to resonate more deeply with your audience.

Maintaining consistency in your brand's voice is important, but so is adaptability. Your brand should be able to retain its core identity while also evolving with digital trends and audience expectations. This balance ensures the brand remains engaging and does not fade into the background noise of the digital world.

By following these steps, ChatGPT can become an invaluable asset in your brand's digital strategy, helping you craft a voice that stands out and resonates with your audience on a deeper level.

Offering Social Media Management Services

When offering social media management services, your goal is to be a strategic partner to your clients, guiding them through the complexities of digital engagement and storytelling. ChatGPT can aid in content creation and audience interaction, yet it's the combination of technology and human insight that truly drives success.

Your responsibilities will include developing a coherent social media strategy that is in line with the brand's identity and objectives, creating and scheduling content, monitoring engagement and feedback, and adjusting strategies based on analytics. Understanding each client's unique brand voice and audience is vital, as is the ability to adapt content and strategies to match evolving digital trends and audience expectations.

The use of analytics is indispensable. It provides insights into content performance, audience behavior, and campaign ROI, allowing you to make data-driven decisions to refine and improve your strategies. Being proficient in interpreting this data ensures that the strategies you implement are agile and responsive to the digital environment's dynamic nature.

In terms of structuring your services, offering a range of packages can cater to various client needs and budgets. These could include basic content creation and scheduling packages, more comprehensive packages that also cover engagement and analytics, or fully customized solutions tailored to specific client objectives.

Pricing models are another important consideration. A **retainer-based pricing** model offers stability and facilitates a closer partnership with your clients, as it involves a consistent set of services over a period. **Performance-based pricing**, linking your fees to specific metrics or outcomes, can appeal to clients focused on tangible results and offers the potential for higher earnings based on your ability to drive success.

Focusing on these elements will help you build a social media management service that not only meets the diverse needs of your clientele but also positions you as an essential partner in their digital marketing efforts.

Engagement and Community Management

Engagement and community management stand at the core of a successful social media strategy. They are essential for fostering a vibrant online presence that connects with your audience.

At its heart, **engagement** involves sparking and sustaining a dialogue with your audience that enriches their online experience. This could mean addressing their questions, sharing insights pertinent to their interests, or simply bringing a moment of enjoyment to their day.

Meanwhile, **community management** is like hosting a welcoming digital space where interaction thrives. It encompasses listening to your audience, responding with care, and building a sense of community. ChatGPT is great for handling regular questions, so you can focus on more detailed discussions. It also helps vary your content, engaging different parts of your community.

You can maintain your brand's dynamic online presence by automating routine interactions and analyzing audience feedback. This, coupled with a strategic approach to content diversification and personal interaction, sets the foundation for a thriving social media community.

Real-life Scenario:

Imagine an eco-friendly store that uses ChatGPT during an Earth Day sale to manage a flood of customer inquiries on social media. This lets their team concentrate on more complex questions, improving overall customer service and engagement during a busy time.

The store set up a system where ChatGPT is integrated with their social media platforms through API connections. This setup enables ChatGPT to automatically handle incoming inquiries, using its AI capabilities to provide timely and accurate responses based on a predefined set of information about the store's products, policies, and Earth Day promotions.

For example, suppose a customer asks about the materials used in a particular product featured in the Earth Day sale. In that case, ChatGPT can instantly provide a detailed description of the eco-friendly materials, emphasizing the store's commitment to sustainability. If another customer inquires about shipping times for the promotional items, ChatGPT can refer to the store's shipping policy to offer an estimated delivery timeframe, thereby managing expectations and improving the customer's shopping experience.

Practical Tips for Social Media Management with ChatGPT

Combining ChatGPT's capabilities with personal insights can make a significant difference in managing a social media account effectively. For example, if you're running an Instagram page for a local bakery, ChatGPT can help brainstorm ideas, like featuring a "*Pastry of the Week*" or sharing stories from satisfied customers. You'll need to give it details about the bakery's products and customer base to generate posts that truly connect with your audience. Every post should highlight what makes the bakery special, using descriptions that draw people in and calls to action that encourage them to visit or order.

Example Prompt:

"*I manage an Instagram account for a local bakery known for its artisan breads and pastries. I want to boost engagement and attract more customers through their social media presence. The bakery has a loyal customer base in the community and is often praised for its unique flavors and warm, welcoming atmosphere. I want to create content that showcases their products, tells their story, and connects with their followers personally.*

Content Ideas:

1. **Pastry of the Week Feature:** Highlight a different pastry each week, sharing details about its ingredients and the inspiration behind it and inviting followers to come and try it.

2. **Behind-the-Scenes:** Offer glimpses into the bakery's daily operations, showcasing the care and expertise that goes into making each product.

Details to Include:

- A brief description of the bakery's most popular products and any special ingredients or techniques used.

- Insights into the bakery's atmosphere and why customers enjoy coming here.

- *Calls to action for each post, encouraging people to visit the bakery or place an order.*

Based on this information, generate a series of 9 Instagram posts. Each post should reflect the bakery's warm and inviting brand voice, highlighting what makes them special and engaging their community of followers. Ask me questions if you need more information."

Tip #1: Create a Content Calendar.

The calendar serves as a roadmap for your posting schedule, ensuring content is distributed consistently and at optimal times for engagement. Use scheduling tools like Buffer or Hootsuite to automate post timings and gather analytics, helping you serve content when your audience is most active.

Tip #2: Manage Engagement.

While ChatGPT can assist in writing replies to common comments and direct messages, personal interaction is key for addressing more complex inquiries or providing a customized response. This blend of AI efficiency and personal engagement fosters a welcoming and interactive online community.

Tip #3: Analyze Engagement Metrics.

By analyzing engagement metrics, you can understand what resonates with your audience, what drives participation, and where there's room for improvement. This ongoing evaluation allows you to refine your strategy, ensuring your social media efforts remain effective and engaging over time.

Key Takeaways from Chapter 12

- A well-planned content calendar is crucial for maintaining a consistent and engaging online presence. It ensures that your brand communicates effectively with its audience at every touchpoint.

- Utilizing ChatGPT to maintain a consistent brand voice across all platforms enhances brand memorability and fosters a deeper connection with the audience.

- Integrating analytics tools is essential for measuring content performance, enabling brands to make data-driven decisions that boost engagement and ROI.

- Establish detailed brand guidelines and regularly update ChatGPT with your brand's voice examples to ensure AI communications remain authentic and aligned.

- While consistency is key, the ability to adapt your brand voice to changing trends and audience preferences is crucial for keeping your social media strategy relevant.

- When providing social media management services, offer packages that cater to a range of needs, from content creation to analytics, tailoring your approach to each client's specific goals.

- To align your services with client expectations, consider different pricing strategies, such as retainers for steady collaboration or performance-based pricing for results-focused engagements.

- Leveraging ChatGPT for routine engagement frees up resources to focus on more personalized interactions.

- Use ChatGPT to analyze feedback and comments for actionable insights, informing a continuous improvement strategy for engagement and content relevance.

- Utilize ChatGPT for brainstorming and creating content that resonates with your audience, tailoring posts to reflect unique aspects of the brand or business you're managing.

- Implement tools like Buffer or Hootsuite to manage post-scheduling and analytics, optimizing content delivery for maximum audience engagement.

- Assess engagement metrics regularly to refine and evolve your social media strategy, ensuring your efforts align with audience preferences and digital trends.

CHAPTER 13: LANGUAGE TRANSLATION

Leveraging ChatGPT for Translation Services

In the expanding global marketplace, the ability to communicate across language barriers is invaluable. Businesses and organizations increasingly aim to engage with a global audience, making the demand for accurate and nuanced translation services more critical than ever. This growing need presents a substantial opportunity for translation practitioners to expand their offerings and adapt to the evolving market.

ChatGPT's ability to understand and produce content in various languages stems from its training on diverse internet text. This makes it an efficient tool for quick translations, creating multilingual content, and facilitating communication in global forums. However, it's important to acknowledge that while ChatGPT shows proficiency in popular languages like English, Spanish, French, and German, its performance in less common languages may not be as strong.

The essence of effective translation goes beyond mere word-to-word conversion; it requires cultural sensitivity and an understanding of contextual nuances. Therefore, while ChatGPT can provide an excellent starting point for translations, the role of a skilled human editor is crucial to ensure the translated content is culturally appropriate and accurately conveys the intended message.

This chapter will delve into identifying effective language pairings and niches within the translation market, emphasizing the importance of cultural awareness and precision in translation. Additionally, it will offer guidance on leveraging ChatGPT's capabilities for efficient translation processes and share strategies for marketing translation services on a global scale.

Selection of Language Pairs and Niches

Each language pair represents a unique market, and every niche serves as a specialized product line within this market. Understanding supply and demand dynamics across these linguistic markets is vital for carving out a successful niche for yourself in the translation industry.

High-demand language pairs, such as English-Spanish and English-Chinese, are the industry's heavyweights, attracting a lot of attention but also harboring intense competition. On the other hand, less common pairs like English-Indonesian or Lithuanian-Portuguese present a different scenario—while the demand may be lower, so is the competition, providing an opening for translators to dominate these niche markets.

Selecting which language pairs to specialize in should be a calculated decision based on thorough market research. This includes analyzing online forums, industry reports, and social media to identify trends, as well as scrutinizing job boards and freelance marketplaces to understand the current demand and competition levels for different language pairs. This strategic approach ensures your choice aligns with market needs, personal strengths, and interests.

Focusing on specific niches within these language pairs further allows translators to refine their expertise. Each niche, from legal and medical to literary translation, presents its own challenges and requires a deep understanding of the relevant terminologies, regulations, and cultural nuances. Specializing in a particular niche enhances your proficiency and positions you as an expert in that field, opening doors to targeted opportunities and clientele.

For instance, consider a translator specializing in English-Indonesian translations focusing on tourism. By identifying a demand for high-quality translations in this niche and dedicating efforts to excel in it, the translator can become the preferred choice for businesses and organizations looking to engage with the Indonesian tourism market. This targeted approach enables the translator to stand out in a less crowded field, attracting clients who value expertise and quality in their specific area of interest.

By carefully selecting your language pairs and niches based on demand, competition, and personal interest, and by cultivating deep expertise in your chosen fields, you can establish a distinctive and successful translation service that meets the needs of a diverse and global clientele.

Ensuring Accuracy and Cultural Appropriateness

Two things matter the most when translating texts: getting the translation right and ensuring it fits well with the culture of the people who'll read it. These are big deals because they help ensure that when we translate words from one language to another, we keep their true meaning and show respect for the culture they're entering.

Think about what could happen if medical instructions were translated wrongly. A small mistake could lead to big problems, like someone taking the wrong amount of medicine. That's why accuracy is super important. It means ensuring that the original message, context, and purpose stay the same in the new language. ChatGPT can help start this process, especially with languages it knows well but can't do everything. That's where you come in, checking over the translation to catch and fix any errors.

Cultural fit is just as important. A technically correct translation that doesn't feel right in the new language won't work well. It needs to avoid phrases or ideas that could be confusing or upsetting in the new culture. For instance, the English phrase "*break a leg*" might not make sense or could be taken the wrong way in another culture. Your job is to steer through these cultural differences, making sure the translation is accurate and respectful.

The only way to ensure a translation is accurate and culturally appropriate is to take a two-pronged approach: initial translation by ChatGPT, followed by human review.

Practical Tips for Translating Content with ChatGPT

In this section, I'll give you some straightforward steps to make sure your translations are accurate and culturally appropriate:

1. **Start with a Clear Prompt**: Be specific about what you need. For example, if you're translating an English manual to French, mention that you need technical terms correctly translated. This helps ChatGPT understand exactly what you're looking for.

2. **Review and Refine**: After ChatGPT provides a translation, it's your job to check it. Look for any awkward phrases or errors and adjust the translation to suit the target language and culture better. You're also aiming to translate meanings and cultural nuances.

3. **Handle Idioms Carefully**: Idioms don't always translate directly. Find equivalent expressions in the target

language that convey the same meaning or feeling as the original.

4. **Keep It Consistent**: Use consistent terms throughout your translation, especially for technical, legal, or medical translations. Creating a glossary for your project can help with this.

5. **Use ChatGPT as a Brainstorming Tool**: If you're stuck on translating a sentence, ask ChatGPT for different options. This can give you new ideas on how to phrase things.

6. **Know When to Seek Help**: If you're not an expert translator, it might be wise to hire a professional editor or proofreader to review your work. They can catch mistakes and ensure the translation is professional and culturally appropriate.

These steps are about combining the power of AI with your own oversight and adjustments. This way, you ensure translations are not just accurate but also meaningful to your audience.

Marketing Translation Services

When venturing into the translation services market, your goal is to become the go-to person for businesses and individuals needing to cross language barriers. This starts with establishing a strong online presence where potential clients can discover and learn about your unique value.

Begin by setting up professional profiles on freelancing platforms like Upwork and Fiverr. In these profiles, it's crucial to convey your ability to translate text, understand cultural nuances, and specialize in certain subjects or industries, if applicable. Testimonials and samples of your previous work can serve as powerful endorsements of your skill level and reliability.

However, don't limit yourself to generalist platforms. Explore niche sites like ProZ.com and TranslatorsCafe, catering to translation professionals. These platforms can connect you directly with clients looking for your particular set of language skills. Additionally, signing up with translation agencies such as Gengo or One Hour

Translation might open up opportunities for projects that align with your expertise.

Your personal website is your professional identity online. It's where you can offer a more in-depth look at your services, share your professional journey, and post insightful articles about the translation industry. Thanks to effective SEO practices, this content showcases your expertise and helps you attract clients through organic search results.

But the effort to market yourself shouldn't stop here. Try engaging with both online forums and offline networks. Participation in translation forums, professional groups, and industry conferences can expand your professional network, open up new job opportunities, and keep you informed about the latest trends and demands in the translation market.

This approach ensures you stand out as a professional translator who brings value, expertise, and cultural insight to every project.

Key Takeaways from Chapter 13

- ChatGPT's training on diverse internet text makes it a valuable tool for quick translations. However, it's more proficient in some languages than others.

- While ChatGPT can provide an excellent starting point, human review is crucial to ensure accurate and culturally appropriate translations.

- Choosing the right language pairs and niches is essential. High-demand pairs offer more opportunities but also more competition, while less common pairs may provide niche markets with less competition.

- Translation accuracy involves preserving the original text's meaning, context, and intent.

- Cultural appropriateness requires understanding and respecting the target culture's nuances.

- Include clear prompts, iterative refinement, careful handling of idioms, and consistency in terminology.

- Use ChatGPT for brainstorming, and consider professional editing for non-expert translators.

- Establish a strong online presence through professional profiles on freelancing platforms and niche translation websites.

- Create a personal website and use content marketing and SEO to attract a global audience.

THANK YOU

Dear Reader,

As we reach the end of our journey, I want to extend my heartfelt thanks to you for embarking on this adventure with me. Your engagement and enthusiasm have been the driving force behind these pages.

If this book has sparked new ideas, offered valuable insights, or simply entertained you, I would be immensely grateful if you could take a moment to leave an honest review on Amazon. You can do so by simply scanning the QR code below:

Your feedback not only helps me grow as an author but also guides others who are on a similar quest for knowledge and inspiration.

Thank you once again for your time and support.

May your journey with ChatGPT continue to be fruitful and enriching.

Felix

CONCLUSION

Ethical and Responsible Use of AI in Business

As we've explored the myriad ways ChatGPT can be a game-changer in various industries, we should pause and consider the ethical implications. After all, with great power comes great responsibility, right? AI, like any tool, is a double-edged sword. It can automate tasks, help generate income, and even revolutionize entire industries. But it can also be misused, intentionally or not, in ways that could harm individuals or communities.

First, let's discuss **data privacy**. When using ChatGPT to interact with customers or gather information, it's essential to be transparent about how their data will be used. GDPR, CCPA, and other data protection laws are not only legal requirements but also testaments to growing public concern over data privacy. So, always ensure compliance.

Secondly, there's the issue of **content originality**. While ChatGPT is a fantastic tool for generating content, it's not a substitute for human creativity. Plagiarism is a serious concern, especially when the AI is trained on a vast amount of text from the internet. Always double-check the content it generates and ensure it meets the standards of originality your industry requires.

Thirdly, let's touch on **inclusivity and bias**. AI models can inadvertently perpetuate societal biases present in their training data. Be aware of this limitation and make an effort to ensure the AI's output is inclusive and doesn't marginalize any group of people.

Lastly, consider the **environmental impact**. AI models, especially those as complex as ChatGPT, require significant computational power, which has a carbon footprint. While individual users have limited control over this, being aware of the issue and advocating for more sustainable AI practices is a step in the right direction.

The ethical use of AI is a necessity. As we continue to incorporate ChatGPT and other AI tools into our businesses and daily lives, let's commit to doing so responsibly. After all, the goal is not just to transform ideas into income but to do it in a sustainable, ethical, and beneficial way. So, as you continue to explore ChatGPT's incredible potential, keep these ethical considerations in mind. They will make you a more responsible technology user and a better businessperson, content creator, and global citizen.

Future Prospects: The Evolving Landscape of AI

As we stand on the cusp of a new decade, it's exhilarating to think about the leaps and bounds AI technology will make. ChatGPT is just the beginning, and the landscape of AI is evolving at a pace that's hard to keep up with. But what does this rapid evolution mean for you, the digital alchemist?

AI's capabilities are expanding. We've already seen ChatGPT evolve from a simple text generator to a tool capable of assisting in a wide range of tasks. As technology evolves, we can expect more sophisticated applications. Imagine a future where ChatGPT can write and manage entire email marketing campaigns, including A/B testing and analytics.

The **ethical considerations** discussed in the previous section will become even more critical as AI advances. The line between human and AI-generated content will blur, making issues like data privacy, originality, and inclusivity more complex but also more essential than ever. Staying updated on these issues and adapting your practices accordingly will be crucial.

The democratization of AI is on the horizon. Currently, high-level AI applications are often restricted to those with the technical skills to use them fully. However, platforms like ChatGPT make AI more accessible to the average person. This democratization means that more people will have the tools to turn their ideas into income, leveling the playing field and creating chances for innovation.

As AI takes over more tasks, **the job market will shift**. While it's easy to fear job loss due to automation, the flip side is that new roles and specialties will emerge. Upskilling to adapt to these changes will be key. For instance, knowing how to manage and interpret AI-generated data could become a highly sought-after skill.

The future is bright but not without challenges. Adaptability and a willingness to evolve will be your best assets. AI's landscape is like a river—always moving and always changing. And just like a river, it has the power to carve new paths and create fertile grounds for innovation. Are you ready to go with the flow?

Call to Action: Your Next Steps

Here we are, standing at the threshold of your future. The possibilities are endless, and the world is waiting to see what you'll create. But before you step out and make your mark, let's discuss your next steps.

Take a moment to **revisit the chapters that resonated** most with you. Go back and dig deeper. The devil, as they say, is in the details. And the more you understand the nuances of your chosen path, the better equipped you'll be to navigate its challenges.

Start small, but think big. You don't have to quit your day job to embark on this journey. Start with a side project or a freelance gig. Use it as a sandbox to test your skills, refine your strategies, and understand your market. As you gain confidence and traction, you can start thinking about scaling up.

Never stop learning. The world of digital alchemy is ever-evolving, and to stay ahead, you must keep your finger on the pulse. Follow industry leaders, read relevant literature, take courses, and most importantly, keep experimenting. In this world, the only constant is change.

Build a network. Connect with like-minded individuals, potential clients, and even competitors. A strong network can provide invaluable insights, open doors to new opportunities, and offer a safety net when things go awry.

Lastly, **take action**. All the knowledge in the world is useless if you don't put it into practice. So, what are you waiting for? Your journey into the world of digital alchemy starts NOW. Pick a project, set a deadline, and get to work. And remember, you're not alone. Whenever you hit a roadblock or need a fresh perspective,

ChatGPT and this book will be here, ready to guide you.

Embracing Digital Alchemy to Unlock New Opportunities

As we near the end of this transformative journey, I want to take a moment to reflect with you. We've covered a lot of ground. Each chapter has been a stepping stone in your path to becoming a digital alchemist. But this book is not a magic wand that will instantly turn your ideas into gold.

Digital alchemy is not about quick fixes or shortcuts to success. It's about the art of possibility, the science of problem-solving, and the wisdom to know when to use each. It's about transforming the raw materials of your skills, experiences, and, yes, even your failures into something valuable.

I've given you 13 different ways to make money with ChatGPT, but this is not a get-rich-quick scheme. Each of these avenues requires further study, practice, and, most importantly, trial and error. The best way to get the most out of ChatGPT—and any tool, for that matter—is by rolling up your sleeves and getting your hands dirty. Experiment, fail, learn, and repeat. That's the alchemist's way.

It's fundamental for you to understand how ChatGPT works and how to craft prompts effectively. This is why I highly recommend reading my other book, "ChatGPT for Beginners: Prompt Engineering Made Easy." Prompt engineering is a very useful skill for unlocking ChatGPT's full potential and is essential for successfully implementing the strategies we've discussed. Without a solid understanding of how ChatGPT operates and how to interact with it efficiently, maximizing the benefits of these opportunities would be challenging.

As you move forward, you'll find that the digital landscape is ever-changing. New platforms will emerge, old ones will evolve, and some might even become obsolete. But the principles of digital alchemy are timeless. They're about understanding your tools and your market, but most importantly, understanding yourself.

What are your strengths? What are your weaknesses? What makes you tick?

So, as we close this book, my final recommendation is to *Embrace the Journey*. The road to success is long and filled with challenges and triumphs. But every step and every stumble are part of your unique alchemical process. And who knows? The next idea you transform could be the one that turns to gold.